TIMELESS WALKS IN SAN FRANCISCO

a historical walking guide to the city

by Michelle Padams Brant

*Cover photo: Hopkins and Stanford Residences, California Historical Society, San Francisco (destroyed, 1906)

This book is dedicated to Sarah, William, and Leonard
and to my parents, Sarah and Oscar

Copyright © 1975, 1996 by Michelle Padams Brant
Fifth Printing, 1996
ISBN O-9611346-1-5

TABLE OF CONTENTS

PREFACE

I have been exploring the nooks and crannies of San Francisco for over thirty years. At first I walked only for my own pleasure. Then I took friends with me. Soon I was guiding other members of the historical profession and the students in my San Francisco History classes. I have compiled some of the walks I developed over the years into this book. Each walk averages one hour. I hope you enjoy your walks as much as I have mine.

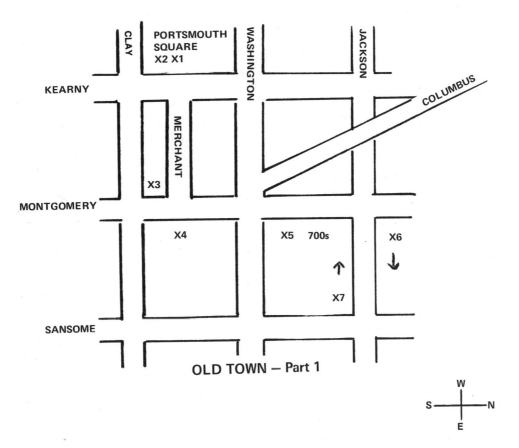

CLAY

PORTSMOUTH
SQUARE
X2 X1

WASHINGTON

JACKSON

COLUMBUS

KEARNY

MERCHANT

X3

MONTGOMERY

X4

X5   700s

X6

X7

SANSOME

OLD TOWN – Part 1

W
S———N
E

—1—

OLD TOWN – Part 2

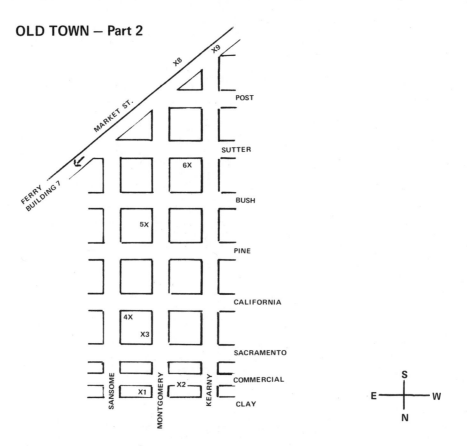

OLD TOWN

Starting Point: Portsmouth Square at the beginning of the bridge to Holiday Inn (map X1). This is on Washington Street between Kearny Street and Grant Avenue.

You are standing on the approximate site where Commander John B. Montgomery raised the American flag on July 9, 1846, and Yerba Buena officially became part of the territory of the United States. Montgomery and 70 men rowed to the landing place which is today Clay and Montgomery Streets. The town at that time contained about 50 buildings and less than 400 non-Indian residents. The *Annals of San Francisco* notes that a portion of the inhabitants watched the flag raising "with tranquility, if not applause." It was around this Plaza that the first schoolhouse stood, the original Custom House was built (to catch smugglers trying to avoid taxes at Monterey), and the first cable car line in the world was later to have its terminus (photo A). Note the ship monument to Robert Louis Stevenson, who lived in San Francisco for a short time.

Note the water line in the picture. Much of the walk today will be on filled land; the original cove was gradually filled in as the city expanded. San Francisco, as the town officially became named in January 1847, was one of the main urban centers for the economic activity generated by the gold rush. People poured into northern California so rapidly that California has the distinction of being the only state aside from the original 13 colonies that entered the union without first going through territorial status; no other state was able to have the required minimum population for statehood in order to do this. The face of the city was to change rapidly with the sudden population influx.

Portsmouth Plaza remained the most important center of the city until 1870 when business activity shifted downtown, and then Union Square became the central plaza. Today's walk will take you in the same direction that the city expanded.

Turn right/south towards Clay Street; here note the plaque (map X2) that marks the terminus of the first cable car line. This cable car line no longer operates and the tracks have been removed. For the centennial celebration of the cable car in 1973, the city did a rerun of the original route of Andrew Hallidie's car in 1873. The original car, housed in the Cable Car Barn on Washington Street and Mason Street, was placed on a truck for the run. Today only three of the cable car lines remain, and they are protected by the National Register for Historic Monuments; you will see models of the original cars in the Cable Car Barn during your Nob Hill walk.

Walk towards the Holiday Inn and go down Merchant Street which is to the right of the Inn. The old Hall of Justice used to stand on the site of the Holiday Inn and you could see the bay from Portsmouth Square. History buffs fought the demolition of the Hall of Justice but lost. Within the Inn is a Chinese culture center on the third floor; the exhibits are often interesting.

Continue east on Merchant Street. At the corner of Merchant and Montgomery the first pony express rider to San Francisco arrived (map X3). In spite of the fanfare, the pony express only existed for 19 months and it was a money loser; however, it did prove the practicality of the central route for the transcontinental railroad.

Across the street, where the pyramid shaped Transamerica building now stands, was the site of the old Montgomery Block (map X4) (photo B). Built in 1853, it was the first four story office building in this area. Many historic events transpired in this building. Editor James King of William died here after being shot by James Casey, a man whose background he had exposed (see the chapter on Mission Dolores for a fuller account of the incident). Sun Yet-Sen, the father of the Chinese Republic, had an office here during his stay in San Francisco. The Montgomery Block survived the 1906 fire, but the general decline of this area in the 1920's and the 1930's turned the building into an artists' studio. Over some protest, the building was razed in 1959 and the lot used for parking until the Transamerica Corporation bought the property and built its pyramid.

The Transamerica Building which was built on the site is a favorite topic among architecturally conscious San Franciscans. Some feel its unusual shape helps minimize its height; others feel that attention catching shapes should be restricted to public buildings and churches. It and the Bank of America headquarters were the tallest buildings in the city. Within the building, on the 27th floor, is an observation floor with a vista view of the city. Note the former Transamerica building on the left where the street ends in a "u". It was built in 1911 and housed the San Francisco born Bank of Italy at one time (now Bank of America). The building is called a "wedding cake" by some because of its appearance and because here North Beach and Montgomery Street meet.

Although most San Francisco streets are parallel to each other, you'll notice how Columbus Street goes off on an angle. The North Beach area that the street leads into was once shoreline (hence North Beach), and the street approximately follows the old cow path out to what is now Ghirardelli Square (some slaughterhouses were once in that area).

Cross over to 716-20 Montgomery Street (map X5). You are now in the heart of the Jackson Square area, designated as a historic district. This is the city's oldest remaining commercial area. It was built on fill to extend the commercial area at Portsmouth Plaza. At first professionals and retailers worked and often lived here. When Union Square replaced the plaza as the center of the commercial area by 1870, these business people left and wholesalers moved in. By the 1920's and 1930's, the area declined. It was rediscovered in the early 1950's by the decorator industry.

You will be taking a walk through only a small part of the district. For detailed information on the entire district, there is no better source than the "Jackson Square Report" by the Department of City Planning (1971). The buildings date from the 1850's and 1860's unless otherwise noted; many are built on filled land, sometimes filled with sunken ships.

716-20 Montgomery: This building, which housed Doros, is believed to rest on the hull of a ship. Large numbers of sailors simply deserted in San Francisco in order to go to the mines (photo C). Real estate was the target of much manipulating and quarreling, and was much more valuable than abandoned ships. The ships were used for a variety of purposes, and fill was one of the uses. The original facade of the building has been covered. Note the plaque across the street which commemorates the first

Jewish religious services held in San Francisco. There has been a small but influential Jewish community in San Francisco from gold rush days to the present, including the founder of Levi jeans.

722-4 Montgomery: This is popularly known as the Belli building after the controversial and well known attorney who owned it. It has been heavily remodeled in a very charming manner though the original building was much more sedate. At one time it housed an early theatre. You can see Belli's office through the window, and there is a lovely courtyard.

726-8 Montgomery: This building once housed a chinaware business, and its sedate appearance is more typical of its period. Note the plaque designating the site of the first San Francisco meeting of a Masonic Lodge in 1849.

732 Montgomery: *The Golden Era* was a popular literary magazine during the 1850's and 1860's, and it published many of the prominent authors of the day, men like Mark Twain. This building was its home. To avoid more buildings like the one on the corner, which at one time housed a Playboy Club, preservationists blanketed the area with a historic district designation. Turn east onto Jackson Street, the street that gives the district its name. Walk on the right while looking on the left (map X6).

498 Jackson: This corner building once housed the bank of Lucas and Turner in which William T. Sherman, of Georgia fame or infamy, was a resident partner.

472-470-460 Jackson: These buildings were occupied by wine and liquor merchants and by consultants in the 19th century.

440-44 Jackson: This heavily remodeled building dates from 1891 in spite of its modern appearance. It housed horses that were used on transportation lines. When horses were replaced by electricity, the building became a car barn for a few years.

400 Jackson: This building dates from post-1906, but it strongly resembles the original office building that stood here. It is a typical office building for the 1850's; as was true in many cities, owners of businesses often lived above the business.

Cross the street and walk back in the direction from which you originally came (west) (map X7).

407 Jackson: This building and the one next to it were the home of the Ghirardelli chocolate factory until 1894; in 1894 the factory was moved to the present Ghirardelli Square.

441 Jackson: The design on the outside of this building has caused it to be known as the Medico-Dental building although no medical offices are known to have been housed here. It was used for a tobacco and coffee warehouse.

443, 451-61, 463-73: These buildings housed A. P. Hotalings wholesale liquor business until 1943. Note the windows. You will see similar window sides on several buildings of the period; they were the "pre-fabs" of their day.

You have probably noticed the use of brick as a building material. San Francisco had six fires in 18 months and brick was resorted to as a means of preserving buildings. The fires also catalyzed the formation of volunteer fire companies in the city, and caused the city to adopt the Phoenix, the mythological bird that rejuvenates itself by bursting into flames and rising again, as a symbol on the city seal. The Jackson Square area was largely spared the 1906 fire and Hotalings headquarters became the focus for a popular jingle in 1906. Some said San Francisco burned because she had been such a wicked city. Those who loved her retaliated:

> *If as some say, God spanked the town*
> *For being over frisky,*
> *Why did he burn the Churches down*
> *And save Hotaling's Whiskey?*

Part of the reference is to the notorious Barbary Coast area that was a couple of blocks from here, around Pacific Street. The term "Barbary Coast" originated around the 1880's and it stood for saloons, dance halls, and brothels. Almost entirely destroyed by the 1906 fire, the buildings were rebuilt to a similar scale, use and appearance. The Coast was not erased until Prohibition, police raids, and the depression killed it. The revival in the area began in the 1950's for the buildings, but the red light district had long since moved to other quarters.

. . . (Switch to map-part two) . . .

Turn south on Montgomery Street and walk to Clay Street. About half a block further west on Clay St. is a plaque of the Society of California Pioneers commemorating their formation on this site in 1850. The society still exists, although to join it you must prove an ancestor from pre-1850 in California. They maintain a small museum which will reopen south of Market in 1997. At the juncture of Clay-Washington, a plaque on the left denotes the spot where Montgomery anchored his ship and rowed to shore (map X1).

Continue south to Commercial Street. This was the site of the Long Wharf, one of several wharves built to accommodate the new business activity. Turn right to 608 Commercial to see the first U.S. subtreasury building. This building has been saved from demolition by allowing the owners "air rights" to cantilever over the building while razing the one next door for the main site of the new building (map X2). The basement of the subtreasury still houses the old vaults. The building currently houses a private museum.

At 650 Commercial St. is the Chinese Historical Museum, which moved here from Adler Street in Chinatown. Returning to Montgomery Street, note the plaque designating where the Hudson Bay Company opened its offices in 1841. The Americans grew nervous over this British activity in the area, but business was not good and the company closed on its own.

When you get to the corner of Montgomery and Sacramento streets, look to your left (east) a few blocks and you will see the site of the long gone Fort Gunneybags of 1856 (on Sacramento Street between Davis and Front). San Francisco hosted three large and well organized Vigilante Committees, two of them in the 1850's. Many prominent citizens took part in these "cleanup" campaigns even though the committees were controversial in their own day as well as now. Some argue the self-appointed law preservers had to do it out of self-protection; others felt there were abuses and punishments fell hardest on disliked minorities like the Chileans. The 1856 Committee was strong enough to hold trials over a prolonged period, and when the official lawmakers tried to break it up, Fort Gunneybags was erected and the Committee survived. Although most culprits were run out of town and/or whipped, a few were hanged. The site on Sacramento Street was also the site where Casey, who shot James King of William, was hanged along with another murderer, Cora.

If this is a weekday (9-5), go into the Wells Fargo History Room at 420 Montgomery St. (map X3). One of the people behind the desk may be free to give you a short tour, but you can go through on your own and look at the clearly marked exhibits.

Exit Wells Fargo, walk south on Montgomery Street, and then turn left (east) at California Street to the Bank of California at 400 California Street (map X4). The history of this bank is very involved with the early development of the city. William Ralston, one of its founders, was San Francisco's most colorful financier in the 1860's and 1870's. He built the original Palace Hotel, a plush tribute to new money. He was heavily involved in speculation in the Nevada silver mines, the mines which financed the second San Francisco boom period after the gold dwindled. He was well known in the city, very involved in real estate, and very much a lover of San Francisco. His speculation became too heavy; because of his intimate connection with the Bank of California and generally bad economic times, the Bank was beset by a panic and had to close its doors in 1875 until feelings calmed. William Ralston walked through the city he loved, took a swim out by North Beach and drowned; whether it was suicide or not has remained a mystery.

The present building dates from 1908 and contains a "Coins of the West" museum. Enter the building, turn to your left, take the stairs down and turn to your right to enter the museum. Here you will find much material about early banking and currency in California, as well as material on some of the more famous personalities of the early city (museum hours: (10-4).

Exit the bank and go to 350 California Street. The Alaska building used to stand there with motifs on all levels denoting the Alaskan trade. The Building was demolished and all that remains are some of the original animal motifs placed on the facade of the newer building.

Enter the Old Merchants Exchange at 465 California Street and go inside the backroom which was designed by Willis Polk. The Hall has been restored to Julia Morgan's original 1903 plans. The former

Trading Hall was headquarters for grain and marine traders during the early days of San Francisco. The maritime murals were created by William A. Coulter, and one by Nils Hagerup. Coulter worked as an illustrator for the San Francisco Call. From 1909-1930 he concentrated on painting, and he is known for his accurate portrayal of maritime scenes.

Return to Montgomery Street. As you walk south towards Market Street you will pass some well known older office buildings. The Kohl building is at 400 Montgomery Street. Willis Polk, an architect who had a role in designing many post-fire buildings in the city, helped restore the Kohl building after the fire. The building has interesting detailing if you look upwards from a distance. 220 Montgomery is the Mills building (map X5). It was originally built in the 1890's and Willis Polk helped in its restoration after the fire. It was built by and named for Darius Mills, a founder of the Bank of California. The size of the Mills building and the Russ building across the street give you an idea of what a "tall" office building was in San Francisco in the 1960's. The steel-frame architecture of the Mill's Building was one of the city's first examples of the "Chicago School" that opened the way for modern high rises.

If you stand at Bush Street and Montgomery Street and look left (east) towards Battery and Bush (two blocks down), you will see the site where the martini was supposed to have been invented in the Oriental Hotel in 1854. Other places in California also claim this distinction.

Cross Sutter Street and turn right (west). 130 Sutter is the Hallidie building (map X6). It was built by Willis Polk in 1916 and named after the cable car inventor, Andrew Hallidie. The building is noted for the decorative fire escapes and the early use of glass. The facade can be separated from the rest of the building if necessary to protect it against demolition.

While you walk back to Montgomery Street, note the gold rush scene on the streetlights. Walk south on Montgomery to Market Street. Briefly note what remains of another Willis Polk building, No. 1 Montgomery, built in 1908.

Look down Market Street to the Ferry building (map X7). Modeled after the Giralda Tower in Seville, it was built in 1898 and survived the earthquake and fire. Many fled to Contra Costa County in the days immediately following the fire via its ferry terminal. Today the building houses a prestigious private club on its third floor, the World Trade Club, and again witnesses the arrival of ferry boats from Sausalito and Tiburon. From Battery (two blocks down) to the Ferry building is all filled land.

Market Street is one of the earliest streets to be planned in the city. Jasper O'Farrell envisioned it as one of the main streets in the city and so marked it as a very broad street in his 1847 survey. It underwent "beautification" in the 1970's with brick sidewalks and trees. Look across to the Palace Hotel (map X8) (photo D). The original Palace Hotel was opened in 1875 by financier William Ralston. It had 800 rooms and it was very elaborately furnished. The hotel was gutted in 1906, and since it had seen better economic times, it was decided to demolish it rather than reconstruct the building.

Walk into the Palace until you come to the Garden Court. This room is not copied after anything in the original hotel but it is so lovely that the city has protected its glass dome with landmark status. In the old Palace Hotel, there was a courtyard where the horses and carriages entered (photo E).

Go back to Market Street. Where Kearny, Geary and Market Streets come together is Lotta's Fountain (map X9). It was dedicated to Lotta Crabtree, a successful local actress, in 1875. The fountain is a favorite landmark and has resisted several attempts at removal. It originally had drinking fountains on the side and a light which was 24 feet tall. The streetlights on Market Street were inspired by those at the Panama-Pacific Exposition of 1915, and in 1916 an eight foot extension was placed on the fountain to make its height conform to the other streetlights. The fountain has been restored; see photo D for an older view of the fountain.

**Photo A — View of San Francisco in 1846-7,
California Historical Society, S.F.**

Photo B — Montgomery Block 1854,
California Historical Society, S.F.

Photo C — San Francisco 1850's,
California Historical Society, S.F.

Photo D — Palace Hotel from Lotta's Fountain in 1887,
California Historical Society, S.F.

Photo E — Ornate entrance to the Palace Hotel, 1890, California Historical Society, S.F.

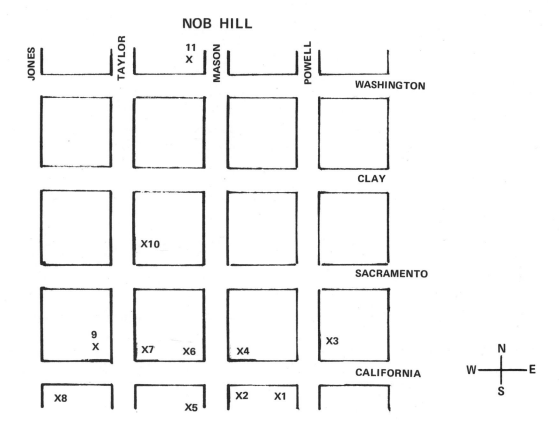

NOB HILL

WASHINGTON

CLAY

SACRAMENTO

CALIFORNIA

JONES · TAYLOR · MASON · POWELL

11 X

X10

9 X · X7 · X6 · X4 · X3

X8 · X5 · X2 · X1

N
W — E
S

NOB HILL

Starting Point: California Street at Powell Street. Take a cable car.

Nob Hill is steeped in the lore of Victorian San Francisco. Although most of the prominent old buildings were swept away in 1906, legend and history have clung tenaciously to this area. At first only eccentrics and those looking for peace and quiet built on the crest. Dr. Hayne built a modest home on the approximate site of the Fairmont Hotel in the mid-1850's, and a few others ventured up here. The rich lived on Rincon Hill which later was leveled so 2nd Street could go through. It was not until the late 1860's that the rich began to look upon this crest as a favorable building spot.

In the 1870's and the 1880's palatial mansions appeared and the area became known as Nob Hill, some say because the wealthy nabobs had come to live here. From this intersection in 1880 you would have been able to view grand homes. On the approximate sites of the Stanford Court Hotel and the Mark Hopkins Hotel you would have seen the imposing Stanford home and the ornate, medieval Hopkin's home (map X1 and X2). The hill bore a railroad stamp in those days, the railroads and the silver mines replacing gold as the source of California's wealth.

Leland Stanford made his fortune building the western half of the transcontinental railroad. He bought this whole block for $60,000 and built a mansion. After twenty years of marriage, the Stanfords had a son and perhaps it was for the boy that this home was built. The boy died at the age of 15, and the home was later destroyed in 1906. What is left to posterity is part of the retaining wall, Stanford University which was built in memory of the boy, and the California Street cable car line which was developed by Stanford and others as a means of bringing transportation to the hill (photo F).

Hopkins, Stanford's business partner in the railroad, bought half of Stanford's lot and built a home on the site of the present Hotel Mark Hopkins (map X2). Mark Hopkins was a modest man, but his wife, twenty years his junior, had elaborate plans. She built a medieval looking structure of wood — painted to look like stone — and had the inside elaborately decorated with murals, marbles, and semi-precious inlaid stones. She seemed to develop a taste for building and decorating and continued to build homes for the rest of her life. Hopkins died before she finished this house and she remarried — to her decorator of course. When she died, she willed the house to her new husband — several years her junior — and after a court fight with the other heirs, he gained title to it. He in turn gave it to the San Francisco Art Association. When the building burned in 1906, paintings were strewn about the lawn of the Flood and Crocker mansions across the street in an attempt to save the art. This was unsuccessful, for those mansions were soon to burn down also. When excavating for the present hotel, a large reservoir was found on the Hopkins property; had anyone known of its existence in 1906, perhaps the old mansion would still be there.

Before you begin walking, note the building at 800 Powell Street (map X3). At one time Stanford had his stables on that spot, but now the sedate University Club is housed there and the building dates from 1909. The empty lot across the street is the repository of several developers' dreams.

Walk west on California Street to the Fairmont (photo G) Hotel (map X4). The Fairmont Hotel stands on the site that silver king Fair was eyeing for his estate. He died before any building materialized, but his daughter and her husband built a hotel on the property. It was almost completed when the fire totally gutted it; the older portion of the present hotel was built shortly after the 1906 fire. Walk inside for a view of its lobby which is done in the grand spirit; note the marble, the deep red velvet, the crest of black wood and gold leaf, the two beveled mirrors from the Castello di Vincigliato. Walk past the elaborate stairway and turn right into the corridor which leads to the outside elevator. Along these walls you will find watercolors of San Francisco scenes, and photographs of the 1906 fire.

Exit the hotel, cross over to the Mark Hopkins Hotel and walk halfway down Mason Street for a view of four buildings designed by Willis Polk (No. 831-849), the city's major post-earthquake designer (map X5). Return to California Street. The imposing brown edifice at 1000 California Street is the Pacific Union Club, a very exclusive organization (map X6). Originally on this site stood the mansion of Mr. Flood, one of the silver kings, but it was gutted by the fire. Willis Polk rebuilt the gutted building along similar but enlarged lines; only the fence is original.

Walk west on California Street to Taylor Street. Where Huntington Park now stands was the site of the Colton home (map X7). Colton came into the railroad partnership later as a legal advisor. Huntington, the third of the Big Four, bought the home from Colton's widow. When the house burned in 1906 the property was donated to the city for a park.

Across the street at 1111 California Street is the Masonic Temple (map X8). Enter the building to see the historical window. The window interprets the history of the California Masons who came by land and by sea; the wayfarers are on the left and the seafarers are on the right. The figures hold fruits and other items to represent the diverse roles masons have played in the founding of California. Eight scenes portray the development of the state. On the seafarer side, scenes show schooners coming around Cape Horn, steamboats, the San Francisco wharf at the turn of the century, and the home of the first Constitutional Convention in California. The central figure represents the master mason. The window contains many other scenes including the All-Seeing Eye, an important Masonic symbol which may also be found on your dollar bill. The window is plastic with materials imbedded in it. On the second floor are display cases and a library dealing with Masonic history.

Grace Cathedral stands on the site of Charles Crocker's home (map X9). Crocker was in charge of supervising the building of the railroad and it was he who imported Chinese laborers for the work. He thus became the target for labor agitators in the 1870's (a nationwide depression had occurred in 1873). His home once became the scene of a mass protest staged by labor. Crocker had wanted to buy the property of his neighbor and felt his neighbor asked too high a price. So he built a tall fence to block his neighbor's view and thus force him to sell. This provoked the mass meeting because labor viewed this action as a symbol of the arrogance of wealth. Ironically, the neighbor was a Chinese undertaker — the very ethnic group that bore so much of the brunt of labor's anger.

When the Crocker mansion burned, the family donated the land to Grace Church, a church which traces itself back to 1849. The cornerstone for this Cathedral was laid in 1910. Enter the Cathedral for a look at the interior and at the stained glass windows. The windows were made by three studios. The Charles Connick Studios did the traditional glass in the west half of the cathedral; the head of this studio was a pioneer in rediscovering medieval blues. Gabriel Loire of Chartres, France, who studied under the impressionist painter Rouault, designed the faceted glass. The glass in the last three nave bays is by Willet Studios in Philadelphia. Both inside and outside the Church is a Labyrinth, a meditation ritual replicated from a 13th century floor at Chartes. Exit the Cathedral on the Taylor Street Side and turn to the building to see the Ghiberti Doors. These doors are casts made from originals in the Baptistry of Florence Cathedral during WWII. They are bronze with gilt panels and weigh four tons. The original Ghiberti doors date from the 15th century.

Continue downhill on Taylor Street to 1110 Taylor Street (map X10). It is rumored that this small place belonged to Flood's coachman and survived the fire. Return to Sacramento Street and walk east to Mason Street. Turn left (north) on Mason Street and walk down to the Cable Car Bar at the corner of Mason and Washington (map X11).

The cable car is the invention of Andrew Hallidie. Legend has it that Hallidie saw a horse slip and break its leg trying to pull a load up a hill; this inspired him to seek a new system for mounting the 40-odd hills of the city. Whatever the motivation, the result was the cable car; it made its first run one cold morning on August 2, 1873, on Clay Street. You will see one of the original cars from Hallidie's fleet on display. The original car which made the first run survived the 1906 fire because it was on display in Baltimore at the time. It was later rescued from a junkyard and returned to San Francisco in 1939.

The cable cars led to the development of the hilltops, just as the routes of early street transportation led to the development of various other parts of the city. By 1891, Stanford had sponsored a line to Nob Hill (the California line) and then engaged in a lengthy patent battle with Hallidie.

The electric trolley line was introduced to the city in 1891, and its first design imitated the cable cars — open ends and a closed center. In 1900, you could see all three at the Ferry building terminal

— horse cars, electric trollies, and cable cars.

The 1906 earthquake badly damaged the old Ferries and Cliff House Railroad building that stood here; the present building was rebuilt after the quake. Only the cable cars that were on the outskirts of town (the 500's) survived. For the 1973 cable car centennial, the cars were renumbered, the California line was restored to its original colors, and a special hand-built replica of a Powell Street cable car was commissioned (the no. 1) and painted in its early colors of maroon and cream. In 1984, the remaining cable car system was renovated.

1906 spelled the end of most of the cable lines. At one time or another there were nine companies operating 21 lines in the city; now only three lines remain and they are protected by registration under the National Historic Landmarks Act. Some cars were turned into "temporary" homes after the quake, and a few exist today as such.

Browse through this museum. Note the stained oak interiors of the cars, and the rub rails for protection against wagon wheels. There are 57 scale models of all the different style cars, and there is a photo display with explanatory notes. This excellent display is made possible through the expertise and generosity of the Railroad Historical Society. When you are through browsing, walk outside and take the cable car (what else!) home.

Photo F — California and Powell Streets in 1880,
California Historical Society, S.F.

Photo G — Porter Mansion 1880's, approx. site of Fairmont Hotel, Bancroft Library

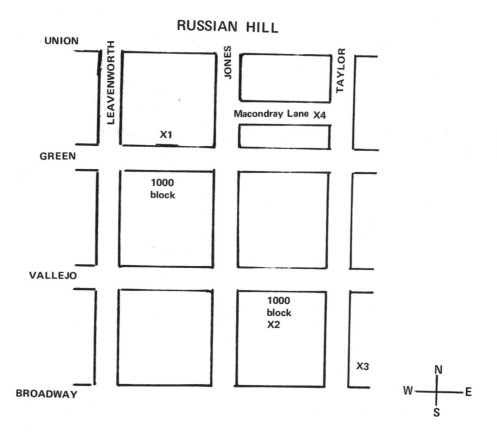

RUSSIAN HILL

UNION

LEAVENWORTH

JONES

TAYLOR

X1

Macondray Lane X4

GREEN

1000
block

VALLEJO

1000
block
X2

X3

BROADWAY

N
W——E
S

RUSSIAN HILL

Starting Point: 1000 block of Green Street. You can take the Hyde-Powell cable car to Hyde and Green Street and then walk up.

Russian Hill's most intimate connection with the San Francisco Russian community is its name! You have to look elsewhere in the city for the Russians. It is unclear how the Russians were connected to this Hill. One version is that the hill came to be called Russian Hill by the early 1850's because Russian sailors who died in this area in the pre-gold rush days were buried at the crest of Vallejo Street. Like most of San Francisco's hills, this was not a popular place to live until transportation became available, and for many years it was a goat pasture. The location of the hill — near Telegraph Hill, North Beach, Chinatown, downtown — guaranteed its popularity as a living area and foredoomed it to the inevitable high rises.

You are standing on a historically interesting block, for before you are examples of several decades of San Francisco architecture (photo H) (map X1). 1067 Green Street is one of two remaining octagonal houses in the city; there used to be five. Octagonal buildings became a fad in the mid-nineteenth century when a man named Orson Fowler "proved" that the shape was conducive for good health. This house dates from the 1850's, although the mansarded roof (flat with a small story under it) and the cupola date from 1880. To see the inside of an octagonal house and the intriguing problem of decorating one, visit the second octagonal house at 2645 Gough Street; it is open to the public, usually every fourth Thursday of the month.

Across the street, at 1088 Green Street, is a remodeled old firehouse. There are several older firehouses in San Francisco which have now been converted to other uses. This one dates from 1908 and served both as a firehouse and as a community gathering spot. It was declared surplus in 1952 and purchased by Mr. and Mrs. Davies; Mrs. Davies maintained it as a private museum and allowed it to be used for charitable and historical purposes. Inside is an old hose cart, and the Knickerbocker No. 5 which

Lillie Hitchcock Coit used to chase as a little girl. Over the entrance is a stained glass window of the Phoenix, the bird on the seal of the city and county of San Francisco. It is also the symbol of the Phoenix Society, an auxiliary arm of the Red Cross. The Phoenix Society is notified of every second and third alarm fire in the city, and its members go to bring blankets, coffee, and other comforting items to the scene of the disaster.

Next to the octagonal house, at 1055 Green Street is a house dating from the 1860's. It is a simple italianate which was remodeled by Julia Morgan — the first licensed woman architect in the U.S. She added the three arches and the iron balcony in 1916. 1045 Green Street has the square bay window usually associated with the horizontal stick style house. 1039-41-43 Green Street dates from the 1880's. It is sometimes difficult to distinguish italianate houses from stick houses. Italianates tend to be more ornate with slanted bays, and stick houses tend to be more horizontal, often with square bays. The two styles sometimes blend, making labels difficult such as in the case of this house. The curved stairway is definitely an individual touch. 1033 Green Street dates from the 1890's and has some italianate features with square bay windows.

The street these houses are on has an interesting history. The man it is named after, Talbot Green, arrived in early San Francisco without his family, as did so many men in the few years after the gold rush. He prospered until a woman recognized him as Mr. Geddis. Subsequent information revealed he had deserted his family in Pennsylvania and welshed on a debt. His name was withdrawn as a candidate for mayor, and he left San Francisco. The name of the street remained.

Walk towards the high-rise apartment at 999 Green Street. This apartment is a graphic illustration of the ongoing battle over height regulations. San Francisco has historically been a small-scale city, and this scale has been threatened. Continue on Green Street and you will see the mix of old and new architecture; compare the wonderful older apartment house on the right behind 999 Green with the ''modern'' 999 version.

Return to Green and Jones, turning left (south) on Jones Street. Walk to the stair ramps designed by Willis Polk. Although this area lay within the 1906 fire limits it managed to survive. The 1000 block on Vallejo Street (map X2) bears the stamp of Willis Polk. Willis Polk and his firm had a widespread influence on the design of new buildings and the remodeling of old buildings after the 1906 fire. 1-3-5 Russian Hill Place, which directly faces you on the left as you stand by the ramps, is Polk in his Mediterranean mood (1915). Walk up the ramp, and to your immediate left is the brick walk into these structures. On the right side of Vallejo street, another architect, Charles Whittlesey, continued the thematic design of Polk at 1085 Vallejo and 1740-2 Jones (the latter visible from the base of the ramps).

You will shortly come to a small alley, Florence Street. This is a charming cul-de-sac in this area. Walk down it, and then return to Vallejo Street. Walk to the end of Vallejo Street, noting the brown shingled homes at 1034-1036. On your right, down the steps, you will see Willis Polk's own home, 1013 Vallejo. Willis Polk designed one of these houses for a client in the 1890's (1019 Vallejo), and built a home for himself on the remainder of the lot. This brown shingle style is also characteristic of Polk, and it is very appealing to modern taste. The three "units" in 1013 Vallejo were originally used by the Polk family, with a tunnel-like connection between the units. The scale inside the house may reflect the 5 foot stature of the architect.

Continue walking down the stairs to Taylor Street. On Taylor Street is Ina Coolbirth Park where you can take a short rest. The House of the Flag used to stand at 1652 Taylor (map X3). When fire swept this area in 1906, the occupant of this house, a flag collector, knew his home was doomed. He planted one of his flags on the roof and fled to the East Bay. When the firefighters came — and some joke they did as much damage as the fire — they saw the flag and assumed this must be an important building. They fought to spare the building and they succeeded. In 1973, the owner applied for a demolition permit, and citizen protest failed to overturn the permit. While demolition had been held up by court actions, a fire dashed hopes of saving the structure. Walk south to 1629 Taylor Street. Built in 1909, the terracing creates a park like feet to this shingle house.

Turn around and go north along Taylor Street past the park. In the middle of the 1800 block, on your left, you will see a set of wooden stairs. Take a deep breath and climb them to Macondray Lane (map X4). Every now and then in San Francisco you will come across a lane like this — quiet, narrow, shady and charming. It is part of the essence that makes San Francisco one of the most beautiful cities in the world. There are several 19th century houses on this lane (such as #15-17), but it is best just to walk it and dream. It will shortly deadend on Jones Street and you will be back near where you began.

1000 Green Street

**Photo H — Russian Hill in the 1860's,
California Historical Society, S.F.**

TELEGRAPH HILL

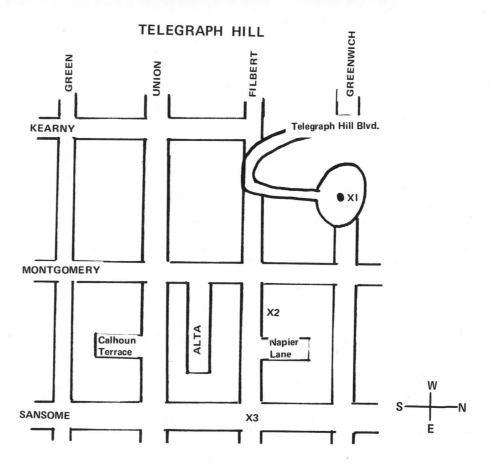

TELEGRAPH HILL

Starting Point: in front of Coit Tower. (Car approach is on Lombard St.)

The hill you are standing on has been known by several names — Loma Alta, Prospect Hill, Goat Hill — but when the firm of Sweeny and Baugh built a semaphone telegraph station here in 1849, the hill became Telegraph Hill (photo I). Two wooden arms would be arranged to announce if a coming ship was a frigate, a schooner, a sloop, or a vessel in distress. The signal for the Pacific Mail Steamship Co. was sure to cause excitement, and news-hungry men would rush down to Clark's Point to await the landing and the mail. San Francisco fog is well known and it caused some obvious problems in this system of announcing ship arrivals. In 1853, this system was replaced by an electromagnetic telegraph line hooked up to Point Lobos.

Residents of the area settled mainly at the base of the hill until the 1870's. In 1882 a German castle-observatory was built on the top of the hill (photo J). Although a cable car line came up to it from 1884 to 1886, the castle never became popular; it burned down in 1903. The structure you are now looking at is Coit tower (map X1). Although its design was controversial when it was built in the 1930's, it has now been adopted as one of the city's landmarks. There is an interesting human story behind this tower. Dr. Coit was a physician who came to the city during the gold rush days. He brought his society wife and his charming little girl, Lillie. When Lillie was young, she had witnessed her mother burning down the old, empty plantation house of Lillie's grandparents in order to drive out squatters and thus protect the acreage. Some say this was the cause of Lillie's growing fascination with fires. Whatever the reason, Lillie was soon seen chasing after the fire fighters much to her elegant mother's dismay. San Francisco had burned down several times in her history as an American city. After the sixth fire in 18 months from 1850-1, various volunteer fire companies were formed, often by those who had had experience fighting fires back east. These were colorful, individualistic companies. The Baltimore boys vied with the New York boys for who would have the honor of getting to the fire first; fisticuffs were occasionally resorted to as competition bred tempers. Lillie's favorite company was Knickerbocker No. 5, and by the age of 16 she was their mascot. Although a permanent fire department was formed in 1866, the volunteer companies, which were also prestigious social clubs, remained in existence and their pre-1863 members became the Exempt Firemen (exempt from military and jury duty). Although Lillie was to travel, marry, divorce and involve herself in many high spirited adventures, she always maintained her contact with the members of Knickerbocker No. 5. When she died in 1929, No. 5 was at her funeral. She left one-third of her estate to the San Francisco Board of Supervisors to beautify the city.

Arthur Brown, Jr.'s firm was given the commission. Brown was a well known architect and he was then in his late forties. He designed the city's Opera House, consulted on numerous architectural projects, and was later to be one of the three advisors on remodeling the U.S. Capitol. He decided on an observation tower because of the hill's history. There was great fanfare about the design, and many artists opposed it. Some said the structure looked like the nozzle of a fire hose. A sculpture of a fireman was also commissioned with the bequest money, but somehow it ended up in Washington Square, at the base of the hill, rather than in front of the Tower.

Go inside the Tower and up the elevator for a panoramic view of the city. Upon descending, walk around the Tower to see the WPA murals. WPA was a New Deal program designed to put people to work doing useful jobs, and preferably jobs in which they could use prior experiences. The Federal Arts Project was a branch of WPA and was geared to creating jobs for unemployed writers, painters, musicians, actors, and researchers. The murals at the base of Coit Tower are an example of what the Federal Arts Project did across the nation in public buildings. The art often had a ''social theme'' and was usually a large work so that several artists could be employed. The murals in Coit Tower represent city scenes and political themes. One of the artists, Rinaldo Cuneo, whose work is in the elevator lobby, came from an old Italian family on the Hill; the Cuneo family is still part of the Telegraph Hill scene.

As you walk away from the Tower and towards the statue, you are in Pioneer Park. After the demise of the signal station in 1870, 22 businessmen purchased the land for park use in 1876. In the early 1920's the road was graded, generally following the discontinued cable car route. The statue of Columbus arrived in 1957 with the usual controversy that attends art commissions. Standing on this hill in 1850 you might have seen the view in photo K.

Telegraph Hill has seen a host of nationalities. Chileans used to cluster near its base, then came the Irish, then the Italians. Younger Italian-Americans tended to move from the Hill in the 1920's to places like the Marina. Now many Chinese-Americans own property in this area; at the base of the Hill, in North Beach, a Chinese grocer runs an Italian market.

Begin your descent on the Greenwich Steps. At Montgomery St. is Julius Castle. In these inflationary times it is difficult to believe that Julius Castle once served lunch for 65 cents. There used to be a car turntable so one could drive up, give the car to a waiting boy, and he would turn the car around on the turntable and park it. Cross Montgomery Street, turn south, and go down the wooden Filbert Steps. The quality of the landscaping and of the neighborhood owe much to the Telegraph Hill Dwellers Association. The homes you pass on your left afford a good example of the simpler forms of architecture of the 1860's and 1870's — 228 Filbert and 224 Filbert are representative (map X2). Turn left into Napier Lane. You are in a different time on this street. The houses date from 1875 to 1890 and the wooden sidewalk was typical of early San Francisco. There are stories about shanghaiing sailors along this lane.

Return to Filbert Street and go to the end of the wooden steps. Rest and look at the view (map X3). You can see some of the old warehouses below. The one with the roof residence and garden is the H. G. Walters warehouse. Many of these old places are now being restored for a variety of business uses. Down by Front and Vallejo was the edge of the old waterfront. Battery Street was once a hill and the site of Fort Montgomery. The Fort was erected 1846-7 at Battery Street and Green Street but it was never used. The hill is now leveled and the Fort is gone, but the name Battery echoes its past.

As you look down, you can see how the hill sharply drops. When San Francisco was a gold rush city, Telegraph Hill was much rounder. Quarrying accounts for the contemporary appearance of the Hill. Rock was quarried here for several reasons. The ships coming here in 1849 and later found it easy to bring passengers and cargo, but sometimes they could not find much to take back with them. Since the hill was so near, they would use rock from it as ballast. As the town expanded, rocks were used for street paving and bulkhead work. Much of the fill for the embarcadero came from the hill. By the early 1900's, there were 14 major quarries in the city. The most controversial one for Hill dwellers was the Gray Brothers Co.

The Gray Brothers were among the earliest cement makers in the city, and they had quarry operations at Telegraph Hill and at Twin Peaks. Conflicts arose with the Hill residents as slippages occurred. There were court battles, but the Gray Bros. blasted away sometimes legally, sometimes illegally. In 1915 a worker killed one of the Gray brothers. The man claimed he thought Gray was going to hit him when he asked for his overdue wages. The man was acquitted, and the sentiment was such against the Gray Bros. that some cheered at the verdict.

Take a deep breath and climb the 248 steps back up to Montgomery Street. Montgomery Street was graded into two levels in the 1930's. 1360 Montgomery Street has interesting decorations on the outside; at one time Hiram Johnson, progressive Governor of California, lived in this building.

Make the first possible left turn to Alta Street. 60 Alta Street is noteworthy because of the Mallard ducks painted on it. The artist, Helen Forbes, was also involved in painting the frescoes at the Mother's House in the San Francisco Zoo and the frescoes in the Merced Post Office. 31 Alta Street is one of the oldest houses in the city; it was built in 1852. Return to Montgomery Street and walk to Union Street. Turn left. Down below, at the foot of Union Street was a Fisherman's Wharf until 1900. Before 1884, the hill was rounder at this point and there were wooden stairs to the base of the hill; quarrying accounts for the sharp drop and the disappearance of the stairs (photo L). Turn right for 9 Calhoun Terrace. The house, which sits setback, dates to 1854; it is an excellent example of Victorian Gothic. Many Telegraph Hill residences were spared the 1906 fire along with this one. Romantic rumor has always attributed this to the Italians throwing wine soaked rags and sacks on their roofs so cinders would not ignite the roofs.

   Return to Coit Tower via the Filbert steps, noting the cascading gardens. As you make the climb back to Coit Tower, it would be nice to recall the Italian contribution to this area. By 1940, Italians were the largest foreign born population in California, and many of these people were in the bay area. Although the census in California is not clear until 1880, it is estimated that there were 300-400 Italians here at the time of the gold rush. There is a joke, told to me by several Italian-Americans, that the miners mined the mines and the Italians mined the miners. Few Italians went into the mines but most went into businesses that fed into the mines; Domenico Ghirardelli, San Francisco's famous chocolate man, began selling candy in the Mother Lode country. San Francisco's Italian population has left its imprint all over the city. St. Ignatius College, now the University of San Francisco, was founded in 1855, and 7 out of 9 of its early presidents were of Italian background. A.P. Giannini, founder of the Bank of Italy — now Bank of America — was an Italian immigrant. After lobbying on the part of the Italian-American community here, the large black Bank of America headquarters in the financial district named their plaza after Giannini, and a stamp has been issued by the Federal government in his honor. Many more Italian names dot San Francisco history, and it is fitting that one of San Francisco's recent mayors was Joseph Alioto. The younger generation began the assimilation process around the 1920's, and moved away from North Beach and Telegraph Hill. Now they are scattered throughout San Francisco and the Bay Area. Yet the Italian flavor clings to this area, and the new interest in ethnic origins has increased the attention of Italian-Americans — intellectually if not physically — to this part of San Francisco.

**Photo I — Telegraph Hill around 1853,
California Historical Society, S.F.**

Photo J — The Telegraph Hill Observatory,
California Historical Society, S.F.

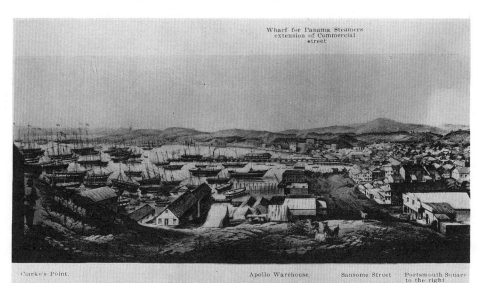

Wharf for Panama Steamers
extension of Commercial
street

Clarke's Point. Apollo Warehouse Sansome Street Portsmouth Square
to the right

View of San Francisco, 1850

Taken from Telegraph Hill in April, by William B. McMurtrie, Draughtsman, of the U. S. Surveying Expedition. Photographed fro
the original in Golden Gate Park Museum with the permission of R. P. Schwerin, owner.

**Photo K — View from Telegraph Hill, 1850,
Bancroft Library.**

Photo L — Union Street Steps (destroyed by quarrying, 1884).
California Historical Society, S.F.

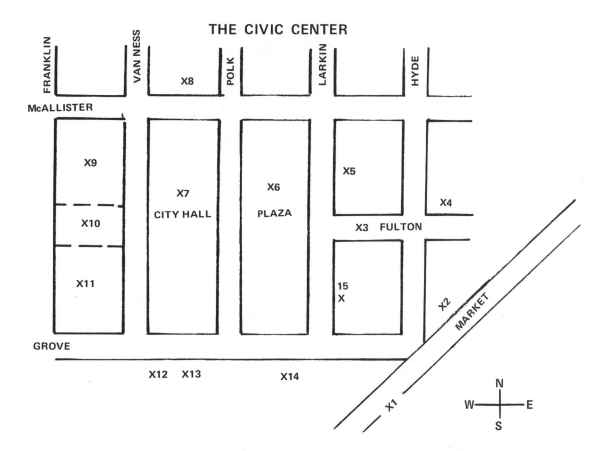

THE CIVIC CENTER

THE CIVIC CENTER:
"San Francisco O Glorious City of Our Hearts"

Starting Point: Start at the corner of Grove—Hyde—Market. If you take BART, get off at the Civic Center stop and use the Grove Street exit. Try to take this walk during the week when the buildings are open.

Standing at Grove-Hyde-Market, you can see two buildings. Across the street, at 1231 Market Street is the old San Franciscan Hotel, which temporarily was used as a city hall (map X1). The ornate Orpheum Theatre (Hyde and Market) (map X2), now utilized as a performing arts center, bears a strong resemblance to the thirteenth century Cathedral of Leon in Spain. With the renovation of the 1920's Paramount Theatre in Oakland, attention was focused on preserving these wonderful older theatres.

Walk north on Hyde to Fulton. You have entered the Civic Center complex. It is one of the most unified sections of the city architecturally. It is done in a classic style with delicate iron fencework. Blue and gold color is located throughout the complex in honor of the state colors. Most of the buildings were constructed in the twenties and thirties because the old civic center was destroyed in the 1906 quake and fire. The buildings are of California granite, which seems to be the American equivalent of marble. The whole complex is dominated by the City Hall. To your right, at 50 United Nations Plaza, is the Federal Office Building (map X4). Arthur Brown, Jr. designed this in 1936. He and his partner Bakewell had a great influence in the design of the Civic Center; Brown was later one of three men chosen to supervise the remodeling of the U.S. Capitol. Inside the center of the building is a small courtyard. You also can see the unfinished backside of the Orpheum Theatre. The city was supposed to create a plan to face the backside in a way that would blend with the rest of the Civic Center. The city dragged its feet, the theatre people spent the money elsewhere, and the backside was never completed.

Go west on Fulton to the large bronze monument between Hyde and Larkin (map X3). You are standing near Marshall Square, once a portion of Yerba Buena Cemetery (McAllister-Market-Larkin).

In 1850 this spot was on the outskirts of the growing city, and the area bounded by McAllister-Market-Larkin was a sandy hill. By the 1870's, the city had expanded and the city fathers were looking for a new site for a civic center; the prior center was near Portsmouth Square in today's Chinatown. This was one of the few large pieces of city-owned real estate so . . . the cemetery was closed; all that remains of the old pioneers buried there is a list of 5000 plus names duly recorded by the California Geneology Society. Mission Dolores cemetery and the cemetery at the Presidio are the only remaining old cemeteries in San Francisco, and burial within the city has been prohibited since the late 1930's except by special permission (which has been granted once).

For a time, this remained a sand lot, and several self-proclaimed orators held forth from here; even the infamous Dennis Kearney of "the Chinese must go" movement spoke here. In 1894, this large monument was erected at Grove-Hyde-Market. It is alternately called the Pioneer Monument or the Lick Monument, the latter after its endower, James Lick. On July 10, 1993, all 1000 tons of this monument were mounted on 28 dollies and moved from Grove-Hyde-Market to its present site to make room for the new library. At the top of the monument is a goddess, probably Minerva, and her crown is a favorite roosting spot for the city's much maligned pigeons. Minerva represents California on the state seal for she was born a woman, and thus symbolizes California's immediate admission to statehood without going through territorial status. The grizzly bear who stands in poor scale behind her was once plentiful in California; it too is present on the rather busy state seal. It is said that General Vallejo, in the early 1840's shot a grizzly on the sand dunes around Fourth and Market.

The four large statues circling the goddess represent different state themes. One shows the miners panning for gold. The second is a goddess with an oar paddling half a boat; perhaps this represents the coming of the '49ers around the Isthmus of Panama or the Cape of Good Hope. Although gold was discovered in 1848, by the time people became convinced it was really a strike, winter had arrived, and so the big rush could not start until 1849. The third statue is of a soldier, a padre, and an Indian; this symbolizes the Spanish period of California when the cross and the sword arrived to make it an outpost of Spain. Wags are fond of either placing a whip in the soldier's hand or a bottle in the padre's. The last statue is a goddess, and she is said to represent Commerce or Plenty.

There are four bas-reliefs depicting western scenes, and five portraits representing men well known to local history:

1. Sutter was a Swiss-German immigrant who established a trading post in Sacramento (which has been restored). Like many here prior to the gold rush, he did not not benefit from the onrush but was hurt by it.

2. James Lick was one of America's Horatio Alger stories, except he arrived in San Francisco already wealthy, 2½ weeks before the gold discovery. He increased his fortune in the old San Francisco standby, real estate. At one point he even owned the Catalina Islands off Southern California. He gave many gifts to his adopted home, among them Lick Observatory and this monument to the California pioneers.

3. Fremont participated in the California phase of the Mexican-American war and later became a U.S. Senator from California. His activities during the war have always remained controversial.

4. Drake was a famous 16th century explorer whose ship, the Golden Hinde, is thought to have landed near Pt. San Quentin, Marin County. A plate of brass dated 1579 was found there and is now housed in the Bancroft Library in Berkeley. Dr. Neasham has claimed to unearth Drake's Fort. A replica of the Golden Hinde set sail in September, 1974, from England to repeat Drake's Voyage.

5. Father Serra was Father Presidente of the mission chain in Alta, California. He is buried in the mission in Carmel.

What remains on the monument is a listing of other important California names. Turn right (north) on Larkin Street to see the former San Francisco Public Library (map X5). This building stands on the approximate site of the old City Hall that was destroyed in the 1906 fire (photo M). The present building was designed in 1916 by George Kelham (who also designed the Customs house on Battery), with a partial grant from Carnegie funds; it is similiar in appearance to the Detroit public library. The old library was a friend to generations of San Franciscans, but as its collection expanded complaints increased about the lack of space and pressure grew for a new building. The old library will become the home of the Asian Art Museum, now housed within the de Young Museum in Golden Gate Park. The Museum will retain the strong architectural features of the building, such as the grand stairway and rotunda, but there is a question about the fate of the five Piazzoni panels whose theme does not fit into an Asian collection. The new library opened in 1996.

Cross the street to the plaza (map X6). The plaza or square is found in several parts of the city, a part of its Spanish-Mexican heritage. Pause for a striking view of the City Hall. The fountain sometimes bubbles, and pranksters occasionally throw sudsy detergent into it. The Civic Center borders a low income area and denizens of the neighborhood are sometimes found sleeping in the plaza. Around 1990, the number of homeless people sleeping in the plaza grew so large that some political opponents dubbed it "Camp Agnos" after the then mayor, social worker Art Agnos. The many flag poles on either side of the plaza each have a bronze plaque which states the flag that is flown from that pole. Among these flags are the 1846 California bear flag, the 1775 flag of the Sons of Liberty, and the first flag of the American Navy.

Continue west across the plaza to City Hall (map X7), which was designed by Arthur Brown, Jr. who designed the Federal Building you saw earlier. On the left is a bronze of James Phelan, turn-of-the-century reform mayor of San Francisco. He appointed a committee to consider plans for beautifying the city; architect B.J.S. Cahill, responsible for some of the ideas later incorporated into the post-earthquake design, was one individual to submit plans.

On the right is a bust of James Rolph, the mayor of the city from 1912 to 1931 (the rebuilding period), and governor of California from 1931-1934. He broke ground for the new City Hall in 1913, and a tribute is paid to him above the clock in the center of the building. He was known as "Sunny Jim Rolph". His aplomb made him a perfect "Mr. San Francisco", and he was a keen politician. People jested that he belonged to a synagogue, a Catholic church, and a variety of Protestant churches.

Walk to the center of the building: the large rotunda and the central marble staircase set the classical tone. Ascend the stairs and walk around the first balcony. Note the clock, the tribute to Rolph, and the leaded windows; the two large windows each contain a ship in the center. On display are the WWI flags of San Francisco's 163rd infantry 91st division; WWI was the last war where hometown boys were often kept together in a unit. The funeral procession of Warren G. Harding, who died while visiting the city, took place around this building.

Exit City Hall, and continue west on McAllister Street to Van Ness Avenue, passing the new court house (map X8). Prior to the earthquake, Van Ness used to be lined with spacious homes. Van Ness was one of the firebreaks in 1906 and many of these homes were destroyed. The Avenue became Auto Row, and Van Ness is designated as Highway 101 (along with Lombard) as the highway goes through San Francisco. In the 1960's, the city decided to encourage residential as well as business use along Van Ness Avenue, and Auto Row has shifted to south of Market. The combination of public transit, automobiles, businesses and residences has not been an easy one. Enter the Veterans Building (map X9) which formerly housed the San Francisco Museum of Modern Art. Various military organizations have had offices here - the American Legion, the Veterans of Foreign Wars, the Spanish-American War Veterans, Daughters of the Confederacy, etc. The United Nations met in this complex in April-June 1945 to draw up its charter. Apropos of this, a statue of George Washington was in the center of the lobby, donated by the DAR; it was removed. The Herbst Theatre is host to various concerts and talks.

Exit the building, turn south and go through the iron gates to the Memorial Court (map X10); this courtyard separates the Veterans Building from its 1930's companion, the Opera House. This restful place teems with activity during opera seasons. Look at the view of City Hall. There are four statues around the entrance door, and some say they represent the burden of the taxpayer holding up the city! Go into the Opera House (map X11). Standing in the foyer, its dome will convey much of the ''feel'' of the Opera House.

Exit the Opera House and continue south to Grove Street. The Louise M. Davies Symphony Hall, designed to blend in with the complex, has a large sculpture in front by Henry Moore. Walk east on Grove Street. The San Francisco Art Commission, at 155 Grove (map X12) has Spanish detailing which seems a bit out of place in the complex. The empty lot next door often contains art exhibits. Continuing east you will pass the Department of Public Health (map X13) and the Civic Auditorium (map X14). The opening of this auditorium coincided with the opening of the Panama-Pacific Exposition of 1915. The auditorium was renamed Bill Graham Civic Auditorium after the Impresario was killed in an airplane crash. Changes are clearly underway for the Civic Center. The ballet building, a center for the blind, and residential units indicates a mixture of use for the area. How this area will be remodeled in the future remains to be be seen.

Photo M — City Hall around 1900,
California Historical Society, S.F.

PACIFIC HEIGHTS

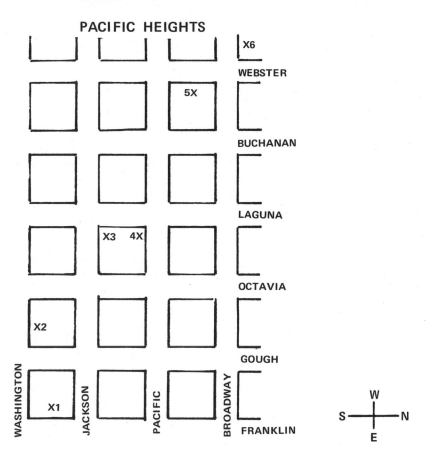

X6

WEBSTER

5X

BUCHANAN

LAGUNA

X3   4X

OCTAVIA

X2

GOUGH

WASHINGTON

X1

JACKSON

PACIFIC

BROADWAY

FRANKLIN

W
S — N
E

—49—

PACIFIC HEIGHTS

Starting Point: 2007 Franklin Street. The California Street cable line stops four blocks from the house.

Pacific Heights — to some the name is synonymous with Victorian San Francisco. Although this is a neighborhood in the process of change, it still contains many fine examples of nineteenth century architecture; it was one of the few areas to escape the 1906 fire. Pacific Heights was annexed to the city in the 1850's as part of the Western Addition; it is now considered a distinctly separate neighborhood from the Western Addition. At one time, this area was mainly greenery—until the late decades of the nineteenth century.

A dramatic place to begin a walk of this area is the old Haas-Lilienthal home (map X1) at 2007 Franklin. This fine home is now the headquarters of the Foundation For San Francisco's Architectural Heritage, one of several organizations in the city dedicated to the preservation of San Francisco's past. In its final days as a single home, a woman in her late eighties and her servants occupied this spacious mansion; when she passed away, her family donated the home for historical purposes. The Haas family dates back to gold rush San Francisco, and represents the German element in that vast influx of population. The descendents of both the Haas and Lilienthal families have been very active in all phases of city life since that time; the Haas family controls Levi Struass Co.

Although grander than many San Francisco Victorians, its exterior contains several of the features that have come to be associated with the word "Victorian architecture". The conical tower suggests the Queen Anne style. The shingling on the house ranges from fish-scale shingles to horizontal shingles. The decorative brackets, slanted bay windows, and stained glass windows are all earmarks of the Victorian era. The house has been restored to its original color; unlike the colorful paint combinations one often sees on remodeled Victorians today, the original Victorian house was usually grey, beige, or cream. The house is built of high-grade redwood; in contrast to modern taste, the Victorians were fond of painting redwood.

The interior of the house has the typical Victorian floor plan with its central entrance, double parlors, and sliding doors. Most of the furnishings are original to the house. The Foundation gives house tours for a modest fee on Wednesdays 12:00-4:00 and Sunday 11-4:30. The tour is worthwhile, and the Foundation should be supported.

Pacific Heights contains a variety of architectural styles. When you are finished with the tour, walk north to Jackson Street and turn left. At 1819 Jackson you will have the opportunity to see what a more restrained Queen Anne of the same decade looked like (1880's). On the corner, at 1901 Jackson, is an example of a later style in San Francisco, a Classic-revival house. This house dates from the early 1900's and has been recycled into a variety of purposes — a school, a restaurant, and currently a retirement home. Several consultates are in this area. The building at 1950-60 Jackson is the German Consulate; it is a Georgian Revival style building designed around 1920. There is a secret passage which connects the two buildings.

Mid-block, on your left, you will see a brick sidewalk going up the hill. Turn left into it. Trees were planted in the center to slow cars. You are approaching the old Spreckels mansion from the back, one of the largest private homes to be built on the west coast. Turn left when you reach Washington Street for a full view of the lovely, French-inspired home at 2080 Washington Street (map X2). It was built in 1912 by George Applegarth who later designed the Palace of Legion of Honor for the same family. It was originally built for the son of Claus Spreckels, the sugar magnate. The Spreckels family was a prominent one in San Francisco society, and its descendents are still around. Alma Spreckels was a character of old San Francisco, known for her offbeat lifestyle and her habit of distributing coins to the poor. After a period of being divided into flats, the home was purchased by Danielle Steel, the best selling author of steamy novels. Her unconventional lifestyle has maintained the house's history of being owned by a character.

Continue to 2150 Washington Street for a fine example of Italian Renaissance Revival architecture. Built in 1915 for the sister of former Mayor and U.S. Senator James D. Phelan, this home retains most of its original exterior appearance. The house was designed by Charles Weeks, who also designed such notable local buildings as the Chronicle building and tower at Fifth and Mission, the Mark Hopkins Hotel, and the Shriners Hospital for Crippled Children. The home served as the site for entertaining both during the Panama-Pacific Exposition and while Phelan was a U.S. Senator. Across the street is Lafayette Square, created in 1867, and the former site of the first observatory in California (erected in 1879).

To get a better feel for the changes in this area, turn to a photograph of this site in the 1870's (photo N). Neither James Phelan nor his sister married. James Phelan died in 1930 and his sister died in 1933. The home was offered for sale as part of the estate, but due to the depression it finally had to be auctioned off for approximately $65,000, less than its original building cost. The house was purchased by the socially prominent McGinnis family. The matriarch of the family died in 1984 in her mid-nineties, having outlived her husband by three decades. The house was purchased in 1985 by a philosophical society.

Turn north on Laguna Street to Jackson Street. Walk across the street to 2090 Jackson, formerly the home of the California Historical Society. This building is an example of Richardson Romanesque which is characterized by massive proportions and by the use of reddish-brown sandstone for the exterior (map X3). This was the home of widower William Whittier, a large paint manufacturer at the turn of the century. The house cost $150,000 to build and the interior has a beautiful combination of woods and marbles inside. The house has had various uses since 1918, but its only controversial use was as the Nazi consulate for a short period. The California Historical Society acquired it in 1956 for $75,000; the Society did some remodeling and refurnished it with period pieces. The Society built a connecting link to its library at 2099 Pacific. Hardly had they completed it when the Trustees announced the Society was in financial difficulty and wanted to sell both houses. You will see the connecting link as you go downhill on Laguna Street. The property is now a private home. As you leave take a close look at the outside and you'll see why sandstone is not a popular building material; it wears away in time.

Turn north at Laguna and go down to Pacific Street (map X4). The two houses on the corner, 2083 and 2099, were built in 1905 for John Spreckels, Jr. 2083 Pacific served as a guest house and Mr. Spreckels lived next door. 2099 Pacific served as the library of the California Historical Society, and now is owned privately.

Walk west on Pacific Street for two blocks and turn right on Webster Street. At 2550 stands the Bourn Mansion (map X5). This massive structure was built in 1896 for William Bourn, President of the Spring Valley Water Company which supplied most of the city's water at the time. It is a very well preserved house, and less than a dozen people have ever lived in it. It was one of Willis Polk's early designs, and has been likened to a brick fortress. Inside are 28 rooms, beautiful woods and stained glass windows. Note the carved wooden entrance doors.

As Webster connects with Broadway, you can see the old Flood Mansion (map X6). 2222 Broadway once belonged to the son of Mr. Flood, the silver king. It is unusual because it is built in marble with wrought copper eaves; marble was difficult to obtain on the west coast and thus is not usually seen in exteriors; granite was used to simulate it. The house, and the two flanking it on either side, now belong to the Convent of the Sacred Heart.

The tour is over for the average walker. For the more energetic, however, a brisk walk up Broadway will take you to the rarified section of Pacific Heights which has been occupied by such well known names as Gordon Getty and Mel Belli. Since so much of the older architecture in this area commands the eye, I'll only highlight a few of my favorites. Continuing west on Broadway will take you to the varied architectural styles of the 2300 block of Broadway. I particularly like 2307, an impressive Queen Anne which Julia Morgan had a hand in modifying. The real hill begins at Pierce, but before climbing it, turn north to 2727 Pierce, between Green and Vallejo. Pierce Street used to be a simple road which, if followed, would lead one down to Washerwoman's Lagoon. The 1866 Italianate Casebolt Mansion, at 2727 Pierce, affords a rare feel of the type of expansive lot some of the Pacific heights homes originally occupied prior to being subdivided.

Return to Pierce and Broadway and continue west. The broad Divisadero Street is considered by some to be the "real" beginning of Pacific Heights. 2801 Broadway, a Willis Polk design, had its moment in the media when its former owner was arrested for his extensive gun collection. 2880 Broadway, also designed by Willis Polk, has particularly fine carved doors; the house to the immediate east used to be independent but was annexed in 1995 to create a music study/hall. 2950 Broadway used to be the home of the colorful attorney Melvin Belli until his well publicized divorce from his former wife, Lia.

Want more? Turn south at the end of Broadway to 2107 Lyon Street (between Jackson and Washington) for the lovely 1895 Swedenborgian Church. The church is based on drawings of an Italian village church, and Bernard Maybeck was involved in its design. You can end the walk by taking a bus on Jackson Street which will bring you, with a transfer, to Van Ness Avenue.

Photo N — The Dunphy Mansion, located at this approximate site in the 1870s, Bancroft Library

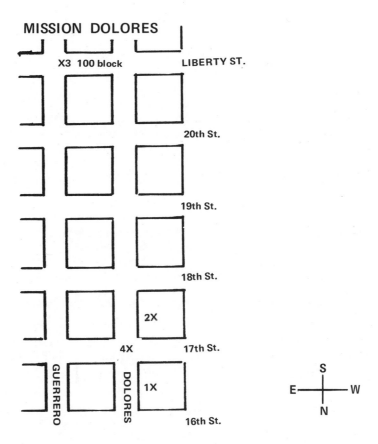

MISSION DOLORES

X3 100 block

LIBERTY ST.

20th St.

19th St.

18th St.

2X

4X   17th St.

GUERRERO

DOLORES

1X

16th St.

S
E —|— W
N

MISSION DOLORES

Starting Point: Mission Dolores (San Francisco de Asis) 320 Dolores Street between 16th and 17th Streets. Take the historic "F" line on Market Street (restored in 1995) to Dolores and walk south to the Mission.

Mission San Francisco de Asis — hereafter referred to as Mission Dolores (map X1) — is the oldest building in San Francisco (if you discount a few old bricks at the Officers' Club in the Presidio). The Spanish pattern of colonial settlement was mission-presidio-pueblo: the religious, military, and secular arms of empire. The Franciscan Order took charge of the mission establishments in what later became Alta California. The original colony in this area was brought up from Mexico by Lt. Moraga and Father Palou. They camped on a lake nearby, around 18th and Dolores, where the present Mission High stands (map X2).

It was June, 1776, a time when the east coast British colonies were preparing to break from England. None of that turbulence could be seen in this area, and on June 29, 1776, the first mass was said; recently this date has become the official birthday of San Francisco. A temporary structure was erected and named after the patron saint of the Franciscan Order. The story goes that St. Francis was not among the names for future missions. "What, is not our own dear Father St. Francis to have a mission assigned to him?" asked Father Serra. The story records the reply, "If St. Francis wishes a mission let him show you a good port and then it will bear his name."

The present structure is from 1791 with some remodeling. The old photo shows the wing which was later torn down for a newer church, and it shows a larger cemetery with only a small fence (photo O). At one time the mission lands covered a much larger area. At its height there were 76,000 head of cattle, over 3,000 horses, living quarters, shops, storehouses (photo P). The mission system in general fell upon hard times when the mission lands were secularized in 1833. Much of the land was sold, and portions of this mission and other missions were leased to businesses.

By 1850, the neighborhood around the mission changed completely. It became a place of bars, horse races, and various pleasure gardens for Sunday enjoyments. In 1857, the Mission was restored to the Catholic archdiocese and the mission area ceased to participate in these amusements. In 1876, the city caught up with the Mission. Dolores Street was graded, cutting off more of the cemetery. 16th Street was extended, cutting off part of the old storage wing, and a newer church was constructed to house the growing membership. As fate would decree, the 1906 quake damaged the new church (the present one dates from 1918) and left Mission Dolores intact except for a toppled pedestal or two. (photo Q)

By 1890, the Mission district had become a living area with a reputation for good weather. Mission Street had long been cut through, approximately following the old road from the waterfront to the Mission. The names of the streets in this area reflect its Spanish past — Valencia, Guerrero — and since WWII, the heaviest concentrated ethnic group in the area has again become Spanish-speaking. Yuppies and other middle income San Franciscans "rediscovered" this area in the 1970's while in pursuit of affordable housing, and they have injected a new element into this area. Since the Mission district was partially spared from the 1906 fire, there are many fine examples of Victorian architecture here. A walk down the 100 block of Liberty Street will give you a condensed view of older homes that have been renovated (map X3).

Stand back from the Mission, restored by Willis Polk around 1920, for a view of mission architecture. The walls are four foot thick adobe, secured by wooden pegs and rawhide (not visible); the thick walls always keep the Mission cool. Other features common to mission architecture are the tile roof, the gentle arches, and the bell tower. The three bells were cast in Mexico in the 1790's.

Walk inside the Mission. As you enter, to your right in back of the church you will see the marker for the grave of Leidersdorff. Leidersdorff was a mulatto who came to San Francisco from the West Indies in 1841. He brought the ship Sitka from Alaska to Yerba Buena; the Sitka was the first steamboat on the bay. Liedersdorff became a prominent citizen in the area, and when he died in 1848 he was honored by burial within the church. There is also a short street in the financial district named after him.

To your left, facing the altar, note the original confessional doors. Look upward as you walk towards the altar to see the archway with its decorative panel. The red, grey, and white chevron pattern was applied in the restoration of 1890. The baroque reredos behind the altar and the statues to the side date from the early 1800's. The ceiling is colored with vegetable dyes just as the Indians used to color the ceiling. As you start up the steps to exit, note Moraga's grave to your right; Moraga was the military man who helped Father Palou bring up the first colony of settlers.

Exit and follow the sign to the Museum and graveyard. You will pass a diorama and old photos depicting the Mission in earlier times. Then you will arrive at the graveyard, the highlight of the tour. This has to be the most cheerful graveyard around. The flowers, the wandering aisles, give this spot a feeling of seclusion, peace and joyfulness even on dreary days. Walk around and read the various stones. Among them you will find many of the original settlers, like the Noe family. Many of the names are Spanish and Irish; the last burial was an Irishman in 1862. Along the side you will find the grave of James Sullivan who was killed by the Vigilante Committee (the "V.C." you see on some of the graves). Don Francisco de Haro, the first alcalde of the village of Yerba Buena, is buried here, along with Luis Arguello, first governor of Alta California; during the 1906 quake, Arguello's pedestal toppled. On the side away from the Mission building, there is a large memorial to another V.C. victim, James P. Casey; "May God Forgive My Persecutors" is engraved on the headstone. Mr. Casey was the editor of a small paper in San Francisco. Editor King was the muckraking and controversial editor of a larger paper. Editor King wrote a series of exposes concerning Casey, and revealed, among other items, that Mr. Casey had served time in Sing Sing prison before coming to San Francisco. When King refused to cease the journalistic attacks, Casey shot King while he was crossing Montgomery Street. King died about six days later, but there was a question whether he died from the bullet wound or from a sponge left in the wound by his physician. Unfortunately, King's death was the spark which ignited the second Vigilante Committee of 1856 and, as a result, poor Mr. Casey now lies buried in Mission Dolores cemetery. Next to Casey's marker is a tall monument to Mr. Murray, a member of volunteer Columbian Engine Co. No. 11.

Although the Indians in the area were Costanoans, the Indian maiden whose statue stands in the yard is Lily of the Mohawks — the Mohawks were an eastern tribe. She was considered for canonization, and the statue is meant to be a tribute to all Indians buried here. The Indian graves are unmarked, and many had been buried in the portions of the graveyard that were paved over. Mission Dolores was not a favorite choice among the Indians — if indeed any of the missions were — because of the cold climate. Indians who fell ill were sent over to the better weather of Mission San Rafael to recuperate.

In the middle of the graveyard, is a statue of Father Serra. Father Serra is the best known of the mission fathers, and was the first in charge of establishing the mission system of Alta California. Serra only founded nine of the twenty-one missions, but he is the best remembered of the mission fathers. He is buried in the mission in Carmel.

Exit through the door by the wall. As you walk outside, look right to the end of the street to see the bronze bell that marks the old El Camino Real, the dirt road that, in a shifting fashion, connected all 21 missions when the mission system was at its glory (map X4). In 1850, there was also a plank road from Portsmouth Plaza to the Mission. The 1906 fire had its southern edge about here. Across the street, Notre Dame Place at 347 Dolores, was rebuilt after the original building burnt; note the old iron gates. 220-214 Dolores was constructed in the 1850's and lived in by the Tranforan family for half a century. After the 1906 earthquake, the Mission area became a temporary home for displaced people. Some remained to build permanent homes. This became a working class area peopled with Irish, Germans and Italians until World War II. The War brought in an influx of newer immigrants; Spanish-speaking immigrants were the largest group, and so Hispanics reclaimed the Mission area. If you walked here from Market, return to Market via Guerrero Street, one block east, noting the various older homes, particularly the well preserved row of homes on the 100 block of Guerrero.

**Photo O — Mission Dolores around the 1860's,
California Historical Society, S.F.**

THE MISSION OF SAN FRANCISCO, UPPER CALIFORNIA

W.Smyth R.N. del

**Photo P — Mission Dolores — early days,
California Historical Society, S.F.**

**Photo Q — Mission Dolores ca. 1898,
Bancroft Library.**

CHINATOWN

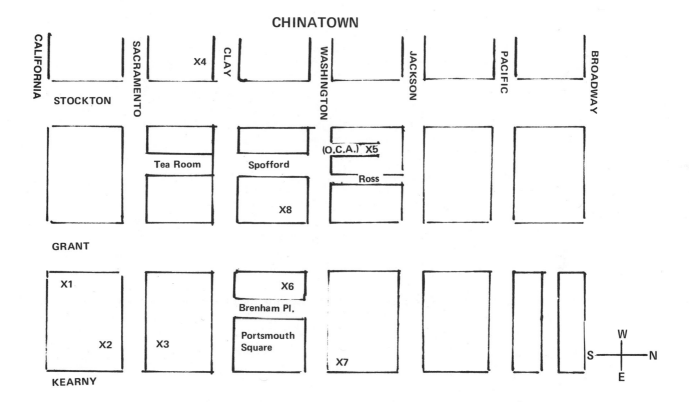

CHINATOWN

Starting Point: St. Mary's Square (660 California Street between Grant and Kearny)

Today you are going to walk through the sights and smells that make up Chinatown — the small fresh fruit and vegetable stores, the Chinese delicatessens and bakeries, the herb shops, the various fraternal organizations, the sound of Cantonese. Sit down on one of the benches in St. Mary's Square to read a short history of the Chinese in California before you begin your walk. This square is dominated by a statue of Dr. Sun Yat Sen, founder of the Republic of China, who spent several years of exile in San Francisco. The sculpture is by Benjamino Bufano.

"He doesn't have a Chinaman's chance" is a saying that is rumored to have its origins in this state, and well it might have. Although there were some Chinese in California prior to 1849, most Chinese arrived here for the gold rush. In 1849 there were 791 Chinese in California; by 1851 this number rose to 10,000. Most of these were Cantonese, and to this day this is the principal dialect spoken in this area. They went to the mines, but although they tended to work only abandoned claims, they were discriminated against with special taxes, and found themselves outside the protection of the law. They were tenacious and as late as 1860 80% of the Chinese here were in mining areas. In the 1860's more began to migrate into urban areas, especially San Francisco and Sacramento; by 1870, 25% of the Chinese here were in San Francisco. They left the city to work on the tunnels of the wineries, to drain swamps, to do seasonal agricultural labor, but they always returned to the city. When the transcontinental railroad was being built, four out of five workers soon were Chinese. Between 1860-80, the Chinese competed with the Irish for first place of foreign born in California. As the number of Chinese increased, agitation against them increased — mainly in the cities. The urban working man seemed to feel particularly threatened by this group.

Language difficulties, poverty, preference, and discrimination combined to keep these people in a ghetto. Up until 1870, these pressures were not insurmountable; one could find a Chinese fishing village at Rincon Point, Chinese companies on the slope of Telegraph Hill, and also around the area of the present Sheraton-Palace. The mid-70's saw a sharp increase in anti-Chinese activity. There was a nationwide depression, and the number of Chinese in California had increased to 65,000. Since the Irish formed the bulk of the union organization in the bay area, it was ethnic against ethnic. Dennis Kearney led mass demonstrations against the Chinese in the 1870's, and a Workingman's Party successfully sponsored state and local candidates pledged to anti-Chinese measures. Provisions were written into the 1879 California constitution against the Chinese. A discriminatory tax was levied against them in the fishing industry in the bay area, an industry heavily Chinese at that time just as it is heavily Italian today. Any Chinese imprisoned had his long braid cut off. From 1850-1872 a Chinese person could not testify in court in a case involving a white man. Chinese children were placed in segregated schools. Ultimately, California put enough pressure politically to prohibit most further Chinese immigration.

Yet the Chinese here survived. Ways of circumventing the immigration law allowed the disparate ratio of men to women to narrow, and the community grew. In the late 19th century, Chinese were dominant in the work force in the canning industry, the cigar industry, the woolen mills, the shoe industry, the sewing industry. And there were always the famous laundries and restaurants. On the positive side, employers liked these hardworking people, and the middle and upper classes of society recognized the cultural achievements of China. Chinatowns were always popular tourist attractions, and even the natives found this self-contained community exotic.

To preserve the familiar and to find strength against discrimination, the Chinese here maintained a strong subculture. Children attended after-school classes in Chinese language and culture, and many continue to do so today. Fraternal organizations aided with problems of loneliness, illness, death and unemployment. Chinese-language newspapers brought news of the old country and interpreted American society for its readers (photo R).

1906 had an important impact on this community. The entire old Chinatown burned. Architecturally it had never been more than small wood shacks. Although there were some attempts to remove the Chinese quarters to a less desirable area of the city, these attempts failed and the Chinese returned to their old neighborhood. In many ways, the architecture you see around Chinatown today is more self-consciously Chinese than anything before the fire. The burning of Chinatown meant other things. For once and for all the myth of subterranean opium dens was disapproved. Also, since most of the city's records were burned, the Chinese in the community who had entered illegally after the Chinese Exclusion Act of 1882, found an opportunity to declare themselves citizens!

WWII is a pivotal point in California for many minorities because of the state's role in war production. Jobs opened in areas formerly closed to minorities. China became an ally and this time U.S. policy won over California policy. Non-American born Chinese were allowed to be naturalized; in 1952 discriminatory immigration laws were erased. Chinese-Americans moved into white-collar and professional positions that had previously been closed to them. Ethnic Chinese immigrants continue to migrate to this area. They face the problems of immigrant adjustment, and they are giving new life to many of the Chinese fraternal organizations.

*   *   *

Across the street from this square is Old St. Mary's Church (map X1). The original church was built in 1854. It is a typical ecclesiastical building for its period; brick had become a popular building material by the 1850's because of the frequent fires. The clock is a favorite landmark to many. It chimes out the hour and above it you are admonished: "Son, observe the time and fly from evil". The 1906 fire demolished all but the walls and the tower. The exterior is very similar to the pre-fire building but the interior has been extensively remodeled. It was the second building to receive city landmark designation. It was in the vicinity of this church that San Francisco's well-publicized self-proclaimed Emperor Norton died. Enter the church to see its stained glass windows.

Exit the church and walk to Kearny Street. Kearny Street is named after a well-known military man who participated in the California phase of the Mexican-American War, and who was military and civil Governor of California in 1847. It is not named after the anti-Chinese labor agitator, Dennis Kearney!

Turn left at Kearny Street and left again at Sacramento Street. Although assimilation has taken its toll, the ornate Nom Kue School at 755 Sacramento (map X2) is an example both of the "new" Chinese architecture of the area and of the role Chinese culture schools continue to play here. The Chinese Chamber of Commerce is across the street from the school at 730 Sacramento (map X3). It participates in the business affairs of Chinatown and organizes the well-known New Year festival.

Go up Sacramento to Grant. Grant Avenue used to be Calle de la Fundacion, one of the original main roads in the early town of Yerba Buena. In 1852 the street became Dupont Street. In 1876, in order to disassociate the street from its popular image as a place of prostitution and opium dens, the name was changed to Grant Avenue between Bush Street and Market Street. It was named after Ulysses Grant who visited San Francisco once! In 1908, the rest of Dupont Street became Grant Avenue to simplify matters.

Cross Grant Avenue and continue along Sacramento Street to Waverly. On your right you will see the Chinese Baptist Church. The original church was built in 1888 and destroyed in 1906. It is only one of many Christian churches in the area. Churches were very active in Chinatown in social welfare areas, and continue to have an influence today. The most famous church in this connection was the Chinese Presbyterian Mission. From this church Donaldina Cameron made her name famous at the turn of the century due to her efforts to aid young Chinese girls sold into prostitution and to combat some of the other social evils in the quarter.

Continue along Sacramento Street towards Stockton Street. If you are hungry, stop for dim sum at the Hang Ah Tea House (Tuesday—Sunday 10—9); it is in the alley by the playground. Inside trays of steaming dim sum will be brought to you. If you have not tried these Chinese delicacies do so, either here or at one of the several other dim sum places in Chinatown. Continue on to Stockton Street. Throughout this walk you will notice how centrally Chinatown is located. The Stockton Tunnel to your left connects this area with the downtown retail stores. Further up the hill you would be on Nob Hill. As the walk continues, you will be on the border of the old Italian section, North Beach.

Turn right on Stockton Street to 843, the Chinese Six Companies (map X4). There are many organizations in Chinatown. Some are family associations based on the family name — the Lee Association is an example. Some are district associations based on the immigrant's home district in China. Both of these were in evidence by 1850. The Chinese Six Companies, formed sometime prior to 1862, is composed of 6 to 8 of the larger districts represented in Chinatown. For a long time it acted as the Supreme Court of Chinese-Americans in California, and before the first Chinese consulate was created in San Francisco in the 1870's, the Six Companies acted as the spokesman for China. In the early years it was also involved in the labor contract arrangements that brought so many Chinese over here who could not afford their own passage. After 1906, the Chinese government sent money to aid the Chinese displaced by the fire. Some of these funds were used to build this "new style" Chinese building. The influence of this organization is not what it once was, but it is still active in Chinese affairs.

Walk towards Clay Street. Turn right on Clay Street to Spofford Alley. These little alleys that are sprinkled throughout Chinatown add great color and mystery to this section. There was a time when shady activities were pursued in these alleys, and when fighting tongs gained ascendency in the 1880's, blood sometimes flowed. Walk down this short street and you will get a feel of the diversity that is Chinatown; here is the Chu Hai University Alumni Association and the Chinese Free Masons.

Spofford Alley ends on Washington Street. Cross the street for another alley — Old Chinatown Lane (map X5). Browse and then return to Washington Street and turn left (east). Go a short distance to Ross Alley. Gambling used to be a major sport here. Lotteries, though illegal, still exist in Chinatown and every now and then are publiziced in the papers because of a police raid. Our business here is more sedate — a fortune cookie factory located at 56 Ross Alley; they usually do not mind if you watch the soft cookies being folded with a fortune inside. San Francisco's Chinatown turns out over 200,000 of these a day. Remember though, this is a business not a tourist attraction, and do not dwell too long.

Return to Washington Street, make a left turn (east) and walk towards Kearny Street. You will pass the Kow Kong Benevolent Association, a fraternal organization at 750 Washington Street. 743 Washington Street used to be an old telephone exchange (map X6). Completed in 1909, it is modeled after a temple in North Lake China. It stands on the spot where Sam Brannan began the first California newspaper, the California Star. Pacific Telephone had 2,477 subscribers to this unique Chinese telephone exchange. People often simply gave the name of the person they wanted. In 1949 this colorful operation went from manual to dial. Then in 1960 the phone company moved and the present Bank of Canton moved in.

From where you are standing you can get a clear view of Portsmouth Square (fully discussed in the chapter on Old Town) where elderly Chinese men sit all day, Chinese children play, and Kung Fu artists practice. Behind Portsmouth Square, on Brenham Place (now Walter U. Lum Place), the Exempt Firemen used to have their headquarters; it burned down with the rest of the section in 1906.

On the corner of Washington and Kearny is the Buddha Universal Church, privately built by its Zen Buddhist and Taoist members; it stands on the site of the old Bella Union theatre of gold rush days (map X7) (photo S). Go into the Holiday Inn at 750 Kearny to visit the Chinese Culture Foundation on the third floor. The Foundation sponsors changing exhibits on various aspects of Chinese culture.

Return to Washington Street and walk west to Grant Avenue. At the corner of old DuPont Street and Washington Street was the first Chinese laundry in 1850, a business that was to grow into a major revenue source for the Chinese community for years. Turn left. At 823 Grant, is a plaque denoting the site where Richardson, the first white settler in Yerba Buena, set up his tent in 1835. Later he built the first wood structure and then the first adobe house on this site (map X8).

Continue down Grant Avenue. At the corner of Grant and Clay was once a murderer's bulletin board. It was also in this area that the first St. Francis Hotel stood from 1851-3; it was reported to be the first hotel in the city to use clean sheets! The Eastern Bakery at 720 Grant sells moon cakes in September. September 15 is the Moon Festival and these ultra-sweet little cakes are given as gifts; it is an agricultural festival similar to the American Thanksgiving.

601 Grant Avenue is the approximate site that Emperor Norton died. In some of the shops you've passed are herbal exhibits. Herb stores have survived both California medical laws — investigations — rulings and the ban on products from mainland China. These stores are finding a new niche with the growing interest in alternative medicine. As a fitting end to your walk in Chinatown, browse through the markets and small supply stores.

Photo R — The Chinese Quarter before 1906, California Historical Society, S.F.

Photo S — Portsmouth Square 1856,
California Historical Society and Bancroft Library

NORTH BEACH
© 1975 by Michelle Brant

Starting Point: The intersection of Columbus Ave., Washington, and Montgomery.

Today's walk is going to take you down most of the length of Columbus Ave., the Market Street of North Beach. Envision this area before the gold rush, a lonely place with sand, shrubbery, rabbits and quails. Apolinario Miranda and his wife Juanna Briones were the first to build a home in this area in the mid-1830's at Powell and Filbert Streets; their home was the third house in Yerba Buena. Apolinario scored another first, both for himself and the area, as the first man to die in North Beach; he was buried in Mission Dolores but his tombstone can no longer be located. Mrs. Briones kept her farm and the people in the area would often be there buying food or renting horses.

The gold rush changed the sleepy pace of the pueblo, and Harry Meiggs changed the face of North Beach. Harry Meiggs, the George Washington of North Beach, arrived in San Francisco in 1850. He bought land around the foot of Powell, the beach area. He became active in local politics and he encouraged the improvement and development of the North Beach area. The peak of his achievement was a 2000' wharf at the foot of Powell (Powell St. ended about 4 blocks sooner than it does today). Meiggs' Wharf was a hub of activity and the first terminal for a ferry; the ferry came from Sausalito. Although the area boomed, Meiggs fell on hard times. To bail himself out of economic difficulties, he took some signed blank city warrants, cashed them, and left town. In time he made money in South American business ventures and repaid his creditors. In 1873, the state legislature tried to pass a bill allowing Meiggs to return to California but the Governor refused to sign it so Harry Meiggs must remain a shadowy George Washington to North Beach.

The ornate Transamerica building in front of you, where the street forms a u-shape, is sometimes called "the wedding cake" because it joins the financial center to North Beach. It used to house the Fugazi Banca Popolare, one of several banks in the city founded by an Italian. John Fugazi's name is well known in North Beach. He came to the area in 1869 and opened a travel agency which also performed side banking functions; the banking aspect of his business grew so large that he began an independent bank. The former occupant, Transamerica Corporation, was a holding company connected with Bank of America; Bank of America developed out of A.P. Giannini's Bank of Italy.

Begin your walk northwest on Columbus Ave. The street originally was Montgomery Ave. but confusion arose from duplicate addresses on Montgomery Street so the city, which was altering several street names in 1909, changed the street's name to Columbus Ave.; I think Meiggs Ave. would have been more appropriate. Envision the cable car line that used to go this area, provided for by an 1861 municipal act (photo T). To your left, when you reach Kearny and Columbus, is Columbus Tower (920 Kearny), one of the few remaining flatiron buildings in the city (flatiron means a building shaped to a triangular site). This building once housed the office of the infamous city political boss, Abe Ruef. Ruef was a brilliant lawyer from a German-Jewish background; he began as a reformer but he became immeshed in corrupt politics. In a series of graft prosecutions around the time of the earthquake, Ruef was convicted on several charges and sent to prison. There he wrote a series of articles on political corruption and reform, and won public sympathy since he was the only one of the offenders to go to jail. Even the editor who crusaded against Ruef turned around and crusaded for his release. After Ruef served his sentence he remained in California and lived on the profits of the real estate holdings he acquired during the aftermath of the earthquake; he lost everything in the 1929 depression and died a poor man.

Continue walking to Pacific. You are in a portion of the old Barbary Coast area, a term which designates the city's red light district of the 1880's. Almost entirely destroyed by the 1906 fire, the Barbary Coast recovered until Prohibition dealt it another blow. There was an attempt to revive some of the Barbary Coast spirit in the 1930's with the International Settlement. To your right, at Montgomery and Pacific, you can see the posts which held the "International Settlement" sign. The area flourished as a nightclub spot during WWII but faded again in the 1950's and the sign was dismantled around 1960.

A short distance up Columbus is the City Lights Book Store (261 Columbus). This was the gathering spot for the Beat movement of the 1950's, and the store was brought to national attention when it published Allen Ginsberg's *Howl;* the book shortly became immeshed in a three-year obscenity trial. Eventually the Beat movement was dissipated as its momentum faded, tourists invaded, and the drug scene brought police raids.

Continue on to Broad Way (the old spelling). If you were standing here in the 1850's you would see a long wharf to your right jutting from the end of Broadway (Broadway ended two blocks sooner then). The wharf was the accomplishment of Mr. Clark who had it underway by 1848. In 1851, a new structure was built at the same location by the Broadway Wharf Co.; once Clark demonstrated that it could be done many wharves were built in the city which later were filled and became street extensions. The Broadway Wharf was the landing spot for many new arrivals to North Beach. They would get off the ship, walk down the wharf, past Meiggs' house on Broadway, past boarding houses and stores.

Less than a block to your right, at Romolo Place, was the local jail from 1851-1906; the Broadway jail held many a citizen in its day, including a few arrested for "fast driving". Four blocks to your left, at 908 Broadway, is Nuestra Senora de Guadalupe, the old gathering place for the Spanish-speaking people of this area. The present church dates from 1912, and most of the city's Spanish-speaking now live in the Mission district. The church stands on the foundation of one of the earliest synagogues in the city, Sherith Israel. North Beach has always been a polyglot area.

The contemporary appearance of Broadway dates from the 1960's. Enrico's Sidewalk Cafe and Keane's Gallery had already nestled into the area when Carol Doda began the topless fad in 1964 which rapidly degenerated into bottomless and coed topless.

Walk northwest to Vallejo envisioning North Beach in the 1870's with its cobblestone and wood streets, horse-drawn carts, and peddlers hawking their wares. Vallejo St. at Columbus is dominated by St. Francis Church. At Grant and Vallejo you can see Cafe Trieste, the old Beat hangout. The church was begun by French city residents in 1849 making it the first Roman Catholic parish church after

Mission Dolores. The building itself has been replaced several times. The present one dates from 1859-60; it was gutted in 1906 and restored by 1913. Bufano's statue of St. Francis was placed here in 1955 but it was exiled to Oakland in 1961 when the priest objected that the statue's large bulk was blocking the entrance and its 12 tons were cracking the steps. The statue was returned to San Francisco in 1962 and placed outside the Longshoreman's Hall on North Point Street. Due to declining church attendance, St. Francis ceased to be a parish church. As you pass 415 Columbus note the old mural on the ceiling. At 450 Columbus you will see one of the few fine quality old street clocks left in the city. The clock was put there in 1908 and legend says it kept excellent time until its owner, jeweler Rocco Matteuchi, died. Then it stopped for a week of mourning and began again. Inside the store is a collection of old pocket watches that might interest you.

Walk to Union. You are now in the heart of North Beach, Washington Square. The property was given to the city by Major Geary in 1850 making it among the city's oldest squares. You might think it peculiar to find Washington Square on Columbus Ave. with a statue of Ben Franklin, but there is an explanation. The square was named in the 1850's before Montgomery Ave. became Columbus Ave. What surer name could the city fathers find than George Washington's? By the time the street's name became Columbus Ave., the Italian element held ascendancy in the area. The Ben Franklin statue was originally on Market St. and no one is sure why it was moved here in the early 1900's. It was donated by an eccentric San Francisco dentist, Dr. Cogswell. He was a teetotaller who wanted people to drink water; you can see the places for water at the base of the statue. The city stopped buying ice for the cooling device in its base so the statue stands simply as a statue and an irony in this wine loving area.

In the 1850's this square was used as a dump and as a stonecutter's yard. Washington Square was leveled by a chain gang from Broadway jail in the 1860's and when Montgomery Ave. was cut through in the 1870's it became a strolling place. Washington Square was originally rectangular but Montgomery Ave. was cut through creating the triangular green spot you see to the left. This triangle contains the bust of a local benefactor of North Beach, Frank Marini, and a statue by sculptor Melvin Cummings who also did the statue of statue-hating John McLaren in Golden Gate Park.

The Square is always a hub of activity and it is dominated by SS Peter and Paul. Weddings and baptisms take place in the church all day long. Also found on Washington Square is a granite survey station of the U.S. Coast Geodetic Survey; it served from 1869 to 1880. In addition there is the statue of firemen commissioned with the Coit bequest money. The statue was scheduled to be in front of Coit Tower and no one is certain how it ended in Washington Square, but it is appropriate enough for a place that was home to many city residents during and after the 1906 fire.

Ringing Washington Square are many older Italian establishments: Bohemian Cigar Store Cafe, Fior d'Italia. In the old days you could eat large meals in the neighboring restaurants accompanied by 10¢ bottles of wine and wandering musicians who played in return for a meal. The Chinese are the new ethnic group that is becoming dominant in the area and it is fitting that Italian-named grocery stores sometimes are owned by Chinese grocers. If you want to sample some Italian culinary delights, walk to Union and Grant for sweets from the Cuneo Bakery, stop for espresso at Malvina, buy focaccia at Filbert and Stockton.

Return to Columbus and walk toward Filbert. You are passing by the site of Juanna Briones' home and farm. To the left, on the site of the Pagoda Palace Theatre, used to be the first Russian East Orthodox Church in San Francisco. A few blocks away was an early cemetery; the first burial there was in 1847, but when a cholera epidemic caused many deaths, Harry Meiggs saw to it that the bodies were moved to the new Yerba Buena cemetery.

Continue to Mason and go into the North Beach branch library. The site was given in 1852 to the Sisters of the Presentation and their Convent School was here for years. North Beach playground was financed by a 1903 bond issue and the library dates from the late 1950's. Finish reading this chapter in one of the library's seats; the old buildings have long since vanished.

From the library out to the old shoreline of Francisco was the approach to the beach which gave this district its name. This area contained a combination of fashionable homes, industries, pleasure spots, and water activities. James King of William had a home here with other prominent citizens before Rincon Hill became more fashionable in the 1860's. William Pfeiffer had a flour factory on Grant and Francisco powered by the first windmill in the city. Pfeiffer's ornate home, sometimes referred to as Pfeiffer's Folly, was also nearby and when Pfeiffer went broke it became first a refuge for alcoholics and then Pacific Hospital. Pacific Camphen Works was in North Beach and manufactured a burning fluid before it fittingly burned down in 1864. Fay's Soap Factory and a contemporary starch factory were other businesses in the area. Breweries liked the location and there were 10 by 1876; one stood where Francisco Junior High School now stands.

It was the pleasure aspect of this area that is best remembered. Meiggs' Wharf, jutting out from the foot of Powell, was the focus (photo U). The Wharf was originally shaped like an ''F'' but the outer L blew away in 1863. The San Francisco Chronicle of 1865 called Meiggs' Wharf the favorite resort for Sundays. Abe Warner's Spider Palace was one of the main attractions on the Wharf. The Spider Palace had outside cages of animals, and the cobwebs inside were so thick it was said you could hang things from them. Warner had a trap door for swimmers; this was a popular bathing area and there were several bath and health places located here. The Atlantic Gardens on Bay St. had vaudeville shows and The Crab House and similar restaurants served good, inexpensive food.

The sea wall was begun in 1881 and finished in 1913. The beach was filled in and the Wharf became land. Its spirit still floats through the district that bears its name. Outside the library you can catch the Mason St. cable car and return downtown, or you can continue to walk the remainder of Columbus Ave. to the remodeled Old Cannery.

**Photo T — Pre-earthquake cable car line at Columbus and Montgomery,
Bancroft Library.**

MEIGGS WHARF 1865.

**Photo U — Meiggs' Wharf at foot of Powell, 1865,
Bancroft Library.**

A FIRESIDE VIEW © 1975

Starting Point: 655 Presidio Ave. at the Firehouse Museum (Thursday-Sunday 1-4)

In 1852 the Phoenix was adopted as the symbol of the city of San Francisco. The Phoenix is a mythological bird that lives for 500 years then destroys itself by fire and is reborn again for another 500 years. It is a fitting symbol for a city that burned down six times in eighteen months during the gold rush days. Predominately built of wood, this city has an intimate acquaintance with fires and firemen.

Buckets were the most common form of early firefighting; at first the buckets were handsewn leather and held about three gallons of water. In the early 1850s, San Francisco households were required to have six each (see Museum exhibit). The buckets were marked in some way so the owners could reclaim their bucket after a fire.

The volunteer fire department was organized in San Francisco in January, 1850. The volunteers were often men with prior firefighting experience back East. The companies tended to divide along geographic and sometimes political lines. The Monumental Company, formed on April 1, 1850, was a Baltimore group. The Empire Company was composed of New Yorkers; their leader was David Broderick, who became both a state and a United States Senator, and who later died in an infamous duel by Lake Merced with Justice David S. Terry (see Bust in Museum). The Howard Company was composed of Bostonians. Some of the city's French members formed the Lafayette Company in 1853; the helmets of the company had a socket on one side for a plume when parading. The Pennsylvania Engine Company No. 12 wore quaker style uniforms.

Mayor Geary formally signed the ordinance creating the Volunteer Fire Department on July 1, 1850. This department would grow to include 14 fire engine companies, 3 hook and ladder companies, and several hose companies before the regular paid department was created in 1866. Volunteer companies belong to a long tradition; George Washington was a volunteer fireman. These volunteer companies were more than firefighting organizations; they were social clubs, and they were intertwined with local politics.

Each company was very proud of itself and loyal to its members. Great pride was taken in the company engine. The first engine came to San Francisco in 1849; it was pulled by hand and then pumped manually. This and other engines were a great source of pride — silver plating, highly polished brass, gilded and painted wood were not unusual features (the Museum has on display an 1849 hand engine, an 1850 hose cart, and an 1855 hand engine).

Companies could be very competititve. Even though the city established loose controls over the volunteer companies, each acted independently. When the alarm sounded, the race was on to see who could be first. Most of this enthusiasm was due to pride, but some of could be traced to the fact that insurance companies often paid a bonus to the first company there.

Firemarks were an old system for designating which company insured a building; most firemarks were of cast-iron and the first one appeared in San Francisco in 1853. Some problems were created as volunteers occasionally fought over who arrived first, and uninsured buildings were occasionally neglected. All firemarks were gone by the time of the paid department.

Enthusiasm frequently outran the local water supply, and firefighting often consisted of destroying the material rather than the fire. Cisterns, at first of brick and then of concrete, were created as early as 1850. The one at Powell and Ellis is the oldest. The first hydrant was established on Battery Street in 1858. The Pilarcitos Reservoir was created in 1862, but an adequate water supply was to remain a problem until more modern times.

Bells were the earliest alarm system in the city. In 1852, the first bell was hung on the old City Hall at Clay and Kearney. The city was divided into eight fire districts and the bell would signal the division. Since bells would also ring for vigilante meetings, legal holidays and other occasions, this was not the best of systems. By 1863, San Francisco had a fire alarm telegraph system between engine houses.

As the city grew, the need for a city operated and financed fire department became obvious; this was a nationwide trend in the 1850's and 1860's. San Francisco's paid department began in 1866 and it was rung in with the new telegraph alarm system. While some of the old volunteers resented the change, most accepted it and some went over to the paid department like their chief David Scannell.

The volunteer tradition did not disappear. In September, 1860, an Exempt Firemen's Organization was formed and the legislature approved it in 1862 (see Museum exhibits). It was called Exempt because those eligible to join it were exempt from jury and military duty; five years of active service in the old volunteer fire companies was the eligibility requirement. 247 belonged, and the company existed as long as they did; all were dead by 1939. The Exempt Firemen were given the old engine house on Jackson St. east of Kearney. When Montgomery Street was cut through, the Exempts moved to the old Monumental Company building on Brenham Place (photo W). The first bell, and perhaps the first engine, were later housed here. The fate of the engine is unclear; the Museum claims it has San Francisco's first fire engine from 1849, but other sources claim it was destroyed in the 1850's or in the 1906 fire. The bell survived the 1906 fire but was about to be pounded into scrap metal. The son of a former volunteer fireman was sitting in Portsmouth Square at the time, recognized the bell, and saved it. The bell was housed in the DeYoung Museum until 1962. The bell was loaned to the Museum where you can see it, complete with a crack from the sledge hammer.

The paid department championed many technical changes in equipment. Although the department began with hand worked engines, it soon switched to steam power and horses. Since these machines were too heavy for men to pull, and since steam was slow in starting, horses joined the steamer. Horses were first used in San Francisco on August 18, 1863. The men grew as fond of their horses and steamers as they had been of the manual engines. Both horses and steamers were given names (one horse was named Abe Ruef) and poems were written about them. Older firehouses were usually three stores, with the top used for storage; sometimes an iron arm extended form the third floor window facing the street for hoisting hay. Although the horses were phased out by 1921, many stories remain from these years. When the horses were old, at first they were sold to peddlers and there are the stories about vegetables scattered as an ex-fire horse answered the call.

From 1917 to 1921, the Department motorized. The last stable on Jackson St. closed on December 31, 1921. The Fire Department encouraged the public to stop saying "firehouses" and to say "fire stations" because they thought it sounded more professional.

The department also experimented with different methods of turning in alarms. In April, 1865, electrically operated fire boxes were placed on corners. If an individual turned in an alarm, he would crank 25-30 times and wait for a noise; if nothing happened, he went to the next box. By 1870, the box opened with a key, a person pulled the hook, and the rest was automatic. The key became the problem because it was usually placed in a nearby store which might or might not be open when needed (see Museum exhibit). The last of these boxes, at the corner of Stockton and Ellis, was replaced in 1904 by a door of glass which a person breaks and then pulls a hook.

The department was challenged with each new blaze, but it was the 1906 fire that presented the greatest challenge and strained every firefighting resource. Chief Sullivan had warned the city that it could not cope with a fire emergency. At 5:14 a.m., Wednesday, April 18, 1906, the San Andreas fault shook, breaking three main pipes to Crystal Springs Lake (a concrete dam built in 1888), and 556 of the 600 batteries of the fire alarm system. Chief Sullivan fell through a gap that had been his hallway and died from the injuries, depriving the city of an effective leader and the man who knew the most about emergency firefighting sources.

The Phoenix rose from its ashes. Due to earlier hydraulic mining in this state, the leading hydraulic experts were living in the Bay Area. San Francisco thus began its auxiliary water system which was completed in 1914. There is a domestic water pipe system and a high pressure system. The larger than average hydrants with red, blue or black tops indicate the high pressure auxiliary system. Cisterns were updated and augmented; they can be identified as a circle of bricks at an intersection and a nearby hydrant with a green top.

The spirit that created the Volunteers had not died. The descendants of the Volunteers are the fire buffs. In San Francisco, it is the Phoenix Society, organized in 1932. It is an auxiliary arm of the Red Cross. The more recently organized St. Francis Hook and Ladder Co. seeks to preserve the old traditions and memorabilia of the fire department. The spirit lingers on. On your way home, try to go by the early twentieth century firehouse at 3022 Washington Street (near Baker). It is now a private home (once owned by former Governor Jerry Brown), one of the creative uses of remaining older firehouses. There remain about two dozen of these vintage firehouses in the city.

Photo V — A Firehouse on California Street, Bancroft Library

Photo W — Monumental Engine Co. No. 6, Brenham Place,
Bancroft Library

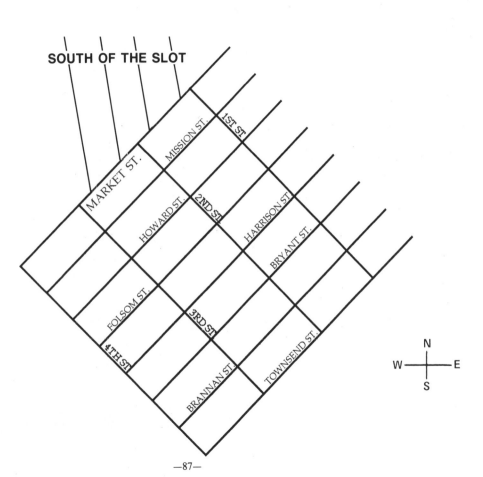

SOUTH OF THE SLOT

MARKET ST.

MISSION ST.

1ST ST.

HOWARD ST.

2ND ST.

HARRISON ST.

BRYANT ST.

FOLSOM ST.

3RD ST.

TOWNSEND ST.

4TH ST.

BRANNAN ST.

N
W — E
S

SOUTH OF THE SLOT

Starting Point: Mission Street between 3rd and 4th Streets, near the Montgomery St. exit of BART.

We will begin at St. Patrick's Church at 756 Mission St. Mission Street was named thus because it followed the old road from the waterfront to the Mission. We are "South of the Slot", the designation for the area south of Market after the cable car tracks were placed on Market St. in the 1880's (paralleled at points by a horse car line). SOMA, as it is now called, has undergone a phoenix like renewal from its prior skid row status. The area became a victim of misguided "urban renewal" in the 1960's and 1970's and many noteworthy buildings were destroyed. At one point St. Patrick's Church was threatened but preservationists won on this one.

Originally built on the site of the present Palace Hotel, the Church was dedicated on this site in 1872. Although largely destroyed in the 1906 fire, the Church was reborn in the older Victorian style. Go inside the Church to see its Tiffany glass windows above the main alter. The green and white marble honors the colors of Ireland. The center window above the alter contains a likeness of St. Patrick.

Exit the Church and go left along Mission St. towards 3rd St. Right next to the Church, to your left on Jessie St., you will see a low, stately brick building with decorative detailing. This is the old P.G.&E. substation built in 1907 with the involvement of Willis Polk. It is now closed to the public so its wonderful marble and arched interior cannot be viewed. The Mexican Museum plans to build on the lot in front.

Continue on to the California Historical Society at 678 Mission (Tues.-Sat. 11-5). Until recently, the Society was located in Pacific Heights in the old Whittier mansion at Laguna and Jackson. The Society experienced financial problems and missles flew back and forth as to who or what was to blame. The trustees decided to sell the mansion and the building on Pacific St. which housed its library. There was some public debate about this action, but the Society went ahead with its plans, and after a short period of limbo found its new home in SOMA. While the current building is considerably less spectacular, the book store and display facilities are much improved. Go inside to see the changing exhibit and to browse through the book store. Joining the Society is inexpensive and confers many benefits.

When you exit the Society you will see a contemporary art gallery across the street. SOMA has long been home to scattered small art galleries, but the opening of the San Francisco Modern Museum of Art at this location has given a major boost to the San Francisco art world, and has helped to lift the galleries out of a recession. Return to 3rd Street and walk southeast to the art museum at 151 3rd St.; the museum relocated here from the Civic Center in 1995. Allan Temko, an art critic with strong views, has likened this building by Mario Botta to the Guggenheim Museum and believes that it has ''spiritual grandeur''. Others have described it in less flattering terms, stating that it lacks warmth and does not highlight the art works. Whatever your reaction, go inside to view its current exhibits and browse through its book store.

Upon exiting the Museum cross the street to Yerba Buena Garden for a look at its exhibits (usually ethnically and locally oriented) and gardens. Then return to 3rd St. and continue in a southeasterly direction, past Moscone Convention Center on Howard. If you pause and glance to your left, you will see three older buildings on Howard which will give you a feel for the type of structures here prior to the latest building boomlet of stores, condos and restaurants. Continuing on 3rd St. you will pass two modern outdoor sculptures on your left (between Howard and Folsom). For once the City Fathers got it right. They require these new buildings to set aside some money/space for art; we are all beneficiaries since a spot of beauty makes life nicer.

Continue on 3rd St. past Folsom towards South Park. In the 1850's, the area bordered by the Bay, Folsom, 3rd St., and Fremont was known as Rincon Hill. The hill was a fashionable residential area of about 14 blocks in what otherwise was an industrial area. In 1869 several prominent businessmen, including William Ralston of Bank of California fame, promoted and achieved a cut of 2nd St. through Rincon Hill in order to connect downtown and the southern waterfront. This cut marked the beginning of the decline of Rincon Hill and its fashionable residents began to move to other parts of the city in the 1870's. Ambrose Bierce, in his short story <u>Beyond the Wall</u>, refers to this area thusly: "I occupied a ground floor apartment in one of a row of houses, all alike, away at the other end of this town, on what we call Rincon Hill. This had been the best quarter of San Francisco, but had fallen into neglect and decay, partly because the primitive character of its domestic architecture no longer suited the maturing tastes of our wealthy citizens, partly because certain public improvements had made a wreck of it." Rincon Hill was further flattened when the Bay Bridge was built. The only reminder of it today is South Park.

When you reach South Park turn left. Suddenly you see a little oasis. A developer, "Lord" George Gordon, planned a residential area surrounding a small park, reminiscent of fashionable London areas. Many prominent people of the day lived here, including the grandparents of Gertrude Atherton (photo X,Y). After the rich exited in the 1870's, the buildings deteriorated. The area burned in 1906 and the buildings were replaced with more commercial structures. One South Park, at the other end of park, is a warehouse built in 1913. In 1935, this area was approved for "soap box speeches" by the Park Commission. In the mid-1980's, however, South Park began a rebirth.

When you reach the end of South Park, turn right onto 2nd Street. We are in the South End Historic District. From gold Rush days to the 1960's San Francisco was a major seaport because of its deep water harbor and sheltered location. This district contains many of the warehouses and industrial buildings that accompanied Port activities from the 1880's to the 1920's; all the old 19th century piers are gone and the shoreline underwent many alterations from the Gold Rush days.

The building styles you will see and the materials utilized vary. Form followed function, changing building codes, technological developments, and land prices. I will not attempt an architectural analysis of most of the buildings, but for those of you interested in this aspect, contact the San Francisco Landmarks Board. Turning right at the end of South Park has placed you near the 600 block of 2nd St. The older buildings are obvious unless grossly remodeled so I will leave them to your observation and evaluation. Most of the buildings on the 600 block were built in the teens and twenties. 634 2nd St. was designed by Lewis Hobart in 1927, and we will end our tour with the Hobart Building on Market St. 698 2nd St. is the S.F. Fire Department Pump House No.1 (there are two), built after the water (or lack thereof) lessons of the 1906 fire; it is designed to pump salt water and remains active though it has now been automated. The Fire Department proposes to move its headquarters to this building from Golden Gate Ave. 699 2nd St., formerly the California Warehouse, is one of the older structures in this area, built in 1882, and was the first warehouse built to allow a railroad car inside the building.

Turn right on Townsend and observe the buildings as you walk towards 3rd St. 123 Townsend was the old Southern Pacific Warehouse build in 1903. 130 Townsend (1906) used to belong to Inglenook Vineyard. 178 Townsend was the home of the California Electric Co. George Roe organized California Electric in 1879, the first electric company in the area. P.G.&E., which formed from some of the smaller electric companies, incorporated in 1905 and became the leader in this field.

Turn right on 3rd St. Numbers 685, 665, 660, and 625 typify the unity that makes this district so interesting; they were built in the 1906-1924 period. 601 3rd St., originally used for wholesalers when it was built in 1913, was also the birth site of Jack London, born in 1876. Turn right on Brannan Street. This street is named for Sam Brannan. Brannan was an early pioneer and shrewd businessman. He is most famous for his short but attention grabbing speech in 1848 when he shouted down Montgomery Ave, holding up a bottle filled with gold nuggets: ''Gold, gold, gold from the American River''. He had a supply store at Sutter's Fort, and some accuse him of delaying the announcement until he had the store well stocked. Thus was the Gold Rush launched, although due to credibility problems, the winter, and the time needed to get to California, the real rush occurred in 1849. Brannan became very rich, was involved in several business ventures, and was one of the chief organizers of the first Vigilante Committee in 1851.

300 Brannan, built in 1912, was a furniture warehouse. 275 and 250 Brannan were built as warehouses about the time of the earthquake. The long, low, odd-shaped building at 200 Brannan was built in

1926 as a freight distributing terminal. Turn right on 1st St. (called Delancy St.) for the most important building in the district at 620-50 1st St., the Oriental Warehouse built in 1867. This was built by the Pacific Mail Steamship Co. This was one of two companies to receive a subsidy from Congress in 1847 to carry the mail between New York and San Francisco, and it began its inaugural voyage with the steamer California in 1848 via Panama (cutting in half the time from the older around-the-Horn route). Traffic unexpectedly increased once the gold rush began. This steamship company brought in most of the 19th century Chinese immigrants to South Beach. The early Chinese immigrants were processed for entry near this warehouse until this function shifted to Angel Island shortly before World War I. The new condos in the background are a clear indication of the changes occurring in this area. A stadium is proposed at the water end of 3rd and 2nd streets, and the evolution of this district is unclear.

Return to Brannan St. and walk towards 2nd St. Turn right on 2nd St; you are on the 500 block of 2nd St. The buildings date from 1906-1923. 555-559 2nd St., built in 1913, was a grocery store/residential building. 544 2nd St. is the Kohler Co. Building of 1923.

At this point you have a choice. If you are tired, return to Market St. via 2nd St. The Hobart Building, designed by Willis Polk and Co. in 1914, with its tower and wonderful detailing, frames a nice end to your tour. If you have remaining energy, however, turn left from 2nd St. via Folsom to 4th St. The Ansel Adams Center for Photography is at 250 4th St. Try also to see the nearby Bufano mosaics at 150 4th St. These are in the lobby of a private building so may not be accessible. The mosaics were transferred here from a downtown cafeteria when the latter was closed.

SOUTH·PARK 1856

Photo X — South Park 1856 West from Second Street
California Historical Society, S.F. G.R. Fardon, Photographer.
FN-00976

SAN JOSE CARS & POTRERO

SOUTH PARK & NORTH BEACH

30

#204

SOUTH PARK IS BETWEEN
2ND & 3RD + BRYANT & BRANNAN STS.

SOUTH PARK 1865.

Photo Y — South Park 1865
California Historical Society, S.F. FN-00677

A BEGINNER'S LIBRARY FOR SAN FRANCISCO HISTORY

American Guide Series, *San Francisco, A Guide to the Bay Cities*

Block, Eugene, *The Immortal San Franciscans*

Caen, Herb (foreword), *Hills of San Francisco*

Gebhard, David, *Architecture in San Francisco and Northern California*

Hansen, Gladys, *San Francisco Almanac*

Junior League, *Here Today*

McGloin, John, *San Francisco, The Story of a City*

Soule, Frank, *Annals of San Francisco and History of California*